LESSONS ON
PRAYER

WITNESS LEE

Living Stream Ministry

Anaheim, CA • www.lsm.org

First Edition, April 1981.

ISBN 978-0-87083-045-7

Published by

Living Stream Ministry
2431 W. La Palma Ave., Anaheim, CA 92801 U.S.A.
P. O. Box 2121, Anaheim, CA 92814 U.S.A.

Printed in the United States of America

13   14   15   16   17   18   /   13   12   11   10   9   8

CONTENTS

PREFACE

This book is composed of messages given during a training by Brother Witness Lee in the winter of 1959 in Taipei, Taiwan.

CHAPTER ONE

THE MEANING OF PRAYER

MATCHING PRAYER AND THE READING OF THE WORD

Psalm 119:147-148 says, "I prevented the dawning of the morning, and cried: I hoped in thy word. Mine eyes prevent the night watches, that I might meditate in thy word."

John 15:7 says, "If you abide in Me and My words abide in you, ask whatever you will, and it shall come to pass to you."

Before we speak concerning the meaning of prayer, let us look at how prayer and reading the Word match one another. The two passages above clearly show us that these two matters—prayer and reading the Word—go hand in hand. In Psalm 119 there is a seeker of God who lives before Him. He matches his seeking for the Word of God with his calling, that is, his prayer, before God. In John 15, speaking of the promise of answers to prayers, the Lord shows us from another aspect how we should match our prayer with the reading of the Word. The Lord's Word shows us that a prayer will be answered on the basis of two things: one is that we abide in Him, and the other is that His words must also abide in us. He promises that if these two basic conditions are present, we may ask whatever we will and it shall come to pass to us. Hence, here it speaks of matching prayer with the reading of the Word.

Brothers and sisters, to a normal Christian, these two things—reading the Word and praying—are the two aspects of his living; both are indispensable. We can see that in God's ordination almost everything in the universe is two-sided. For example, above and below, left and right, yes and no, day and night, male and female—all are two-sided, or you may say they are counterparts for full and proper function.

Our human body gives us many examples of this. For instance, I have two legs which make it very convenient for me to either stand or walk. Suppose I had only one leg. Then I would not be able to stand well, and I would have even more trouble walking. Not only so, but our hands, ears, eyes, and nostrils are also in pairs and symmetrically arranged. The practical living of a Christian before the Lord also has two sides: one side is the reading of the Word, and the other side is prayer. When we walk, we must use both feet simultaneously in order to maintain our balance. We should not walk twenty steps with our right foot and only two steps with our left foot. As a Christian living before God, we also need to read the Word and pray simultaneously, thus keeping the balance.

Unfortunately, however, once God's ordained laws get into our hands we often make them one-sided. God ordains that a Christian should give equal importance to both reading the Word and prayer. Nevertheless, some brothers and sisters enjoy only reading the Scriptures, but not praying. When they read the Bible, they may bury their head in it from morning to evening; the more they read it, the better it tastes. Every page of their Bible has been drawn with many lines—some heavy, some light, some red, and some blue; the whole book is nearly filled with lines. Some have marked two or three copies of the Bible, though they have been saved for only four years. But strangely, they pray very little, and sometimes even when they are moved by the Holy Spirit, they still will not pray. The enjoyment is unlimited when they read the Word, but when they pray it is like taking bitter medicine. On the other hand, there are some who just enjoy praying. The minute they kneel down they are moved to tears, and may sing spiritual songs. They feel so marvelous and energetic when they pray. But if you want them to read the Bible, they immediately doze off. They would rather pray daily than read the Word. You see, again, this is one-sided.

Brothers and sisters, if someone reads the Bible more than he prays he will often fall into letters and regulations which bring a dead, dry spiritual condition. But one who leans to the other side and prays more than he reads the Bible will become spiritually unbalanced. If we want to maintain a normal Christian life, we must give equal attention to both reading the Word and prayer. Just as we use both feet equally when we walk, we should always both read and pray, pray and read. Whenever we pray we must touch the Word of God, and whenever we read the Scriptures we must match it with prayer.

May we look at an illustration confirming this matter. In Ephesians 5, from verse 18 through verse 20, immediately after it says we should be filled with the Spirit, it tells us that we should speak to one another in psalms and hymns and spiritual songs, singing and psalming with our heart to the Lord, and give thanks always for all things in the name of our Lord to God. Again, in Colossians 3:16 and 17, after it says we should let the word of Christ dwell in us richly, it goes on to tell us that we should sing psalms, hymns, and spiritual songs with grace unto God and in all things give thanks to God in the name of the Lord. While both portions of the Word speak of how Christians praise and thank God, the reasons they do so are different. One is due to the infilling of the Spirit, while the other is due to the infilling of the Lord's Word. By comparing these two portions of the Scriptures, you can see that both the reading of the Word and prayer are something which men experience in the Spirit. You can never separate the Word from the Spirit. For the Word is the embodiment of the Spirit, and the Spirit is deposited in the Word. Under normal circumstances, whenever you have the infilling of the words of the Bible, you also have the infilling of the Spirit. And once you are filled with the Spirit, you cannot help but pray. There are various forms of prayer, such as giving thanks to God, blessing God, singing praises to God, weeping and calling before God, fasting and supplicating before God, etc. All these prayers are due to the Spirit's moving within man. When you touch the Word, you will surely know the presence of the Spirit within you. Once you realize the presence of the Spirit, you cannot help but pray;

otherwise, you are one who quenches the Spirit. Hence, we must always match our reading with prayer.

On the contrary, if you pray but do not read the Scriptures or touch the Word of the Lord, your prayer will inevitably come out of your own idea, thought, view, opinion, and inclination. In order to pray out from the Spirit and not out from yourself, you must have the Lord's Word. Now, you can understand why in John 15:7 the Lord Jesus first says, "If you abide in Me and My words abide in you;" then He says, "Ask whatever you will, and it shall come to pass to you." These words show us that if a man learns to always fellowship with the Lord and live in the Lord, His Word will abide in him. One who reads the Word properly is one who abides in the Lord. One who abides outside the Lord is definitely not able to read the Word spiritually; the best he can do is to exercise his mentality to understand; he can never use his spirit to touch the Word. One who abides in the Lord, however, can easily have the Lord's word abiding in him. Since the Lord's word thus abides in him, he cannot help but touch the Spirit, for the Lord's word is spirit. And once he is filled with the Spirit of the Lord, he cannot help but pray. The Lord promises that whatever such a one shall ask, it shall come to pass to him, for at this point, whatever he desires in his heart is not of himself but of the Lord's word and His Spirit—that is the Lord Himself. Hence, in order to have the proper prayer, you must first have the proper reading of the Word.

Therefore, brothers and sisters, proper reading of the Word is surely accompanied by prayer, and proper prayers will surely issue forth from the reading of the Word. Both matters are equally important; neither should be unduly stressed. Moreover, it is also not possible to decide which of the two should be first; they must go hand in hand. When we read the Lord's word in John 15:7, it seems that we should first read the Word and then pray. But in Psalm 119 it says, "I prevented the dawning of the morning, and cried: I hoped in thy word." That seems to indicate that prayer comes before reading the Word. Therefore, it is not necessary to make a rigid decision concerning these two matters; you just need to allow them to proceed in a spontaneous way.

People have often asked me, "Brother Lee, during morning watch, is it better to read the Bible first and then pray or pray first and then read the Bible?" This is hard to answer. I have been living many years, but to this day whenever I walk I am still not certain whether I should start with my right foot or with my left. May I ask you, are you certain? This morning when you rose up and started to walk, did you start with your right foot or with your left? If there is someone who whenever he starts walking would first consider whether to start with the right foot or the left, you would surely suspect that he is a mental case. Whenever we walk, we just do it naturally without caring whether the right or left foot goes first. Please remember, it is also unnecessary for you to decide every morning before the Lord whether to read first and then pray or vice versa. Just remain before the Lord in a normal way. Sometimes you may read the Word first and then pray, while other times you may pray first and then read the Word. You do not need to set up a dead regulation. Sometimes after rising in the morning, you may simply pray a few sentences first and then read the Bible. But other times you may have an inner desire to open the Word and read a few sentences; following the reading, the feelings may come and then you may start to pray. These two things usually occur the same number of times and occupy the same length of time. For the purpose of illustration, let us cite Brother Müller, who operated an orphanage in Great Britain. He was someone in the last century who prayed and read, read and prayed. In his autobiography he told us that every morning he spent some time to draw near to God. You cannot say that during that time he was only reading the Word, nor can you say that he was only praying. In his coming before the Lord every morning he gave equal attention to both reading and praying and kept both in balance. Hence, almost everyone acknowledges that, with regard to the practical aspect of reading and praying, during the last century Müller was the most normal example. He did not have the problem of being one-sided. He was one who used his mind to understand the Bible and exercised his spirit to contact the Word. Furthermore, he was also one who matched his reading with praying.

Therefore, he was very living and fresh, as well as steady and solid before the Lord. Brothers and sisters, I wish to ask you to first give attention to this matter before we go on to the lessons of prayer.

THE MEANING OF PRAYER

Now we may come to the first lesson of prayer—the meaning of prayer. May I ask you, brothers and sisters, what is prayer? What is prayer all about? What is the meaning of prayer? Many people, upon hearing the term prayer, immediately think that it means man coming before God to make supplication. Because man is in want and needs material supply, or is sick and needs healing, or has other problems and needs some solution, he goes before God asking Him to supply his needs, heal his sickness, and solve his problems. Men consider these as prayers. Apparently, there are examples of such prayers in the Bible. For example, the widow in Luke 18 continually went to the judge asking him to avenge her of her grievance. However, brothers and sisters, please remember that this is not the proper meaning of prayer as it is revealed in the Bible. We dare not say that such a definition is wrong, but it is too superficial and lacks both depth and accuracy. If we desire to know what real prayer is today, we must clearly realize that it is not man merely making supplications before God for his own needs.

We know that we should not judge any truth of the Bible merely on the basis of a single passage or aspect. In the same way, you cannot tell what a house looks like simply by one of its corners or rooms. You need to view it from various sides as a whole, and then you will be able to make an accurate judgment. In the same principle, if we collect all the Bible passages concerning prayer and view them as a whole, we will see that prayer is not just a matter of man making supplication to God because he has some needs. This may be partially the meaning of prayer but not entirely. If we have the time, we should gather all the specific examples of prayer in the Bible. For example, in the Old Testament there are the prayers of Abraham, Moses, David, Solomon, Nehemiah, Elijah, Isaiah, Daniel, and others, while in the New Testament there are the prayers of the Lord Jesus and of the disciples. If we study every one of these prayers and look at them as a composite, we will be able to see clearly what prayer is all about. It is not the intention of this writing to study them in such a detailed way; we will only use a simple word to speak concerning the meaning of prayer.

I. PRAYER IS THE MUTUAL CONTACT BETWEEN MAN AND GOD

Prayer is not just man contacting God; it is the mutual contact between man and God. This matter of the contact between God and man is a very great subject in the Bible. We have often said that the purpose of man's living is to be God's vessel. In the universe God is man's content, and man is God's container. Without man, God has no place to put Himself—He becomes a homeless God. I do not understand why this is so, but I know that it is a fact. In the universe God's greatest need is man. God as an entity in Himself is complete, but as far as His operation in the universe is concerned, He still needs man to fulfill that operation.

By this you can understand the last sentence of Ephesians 1, which says that the church is the Body of Christ, the *fullness* of Christ. The term fullness is very hard to translate. It not only denotes the fullness of Christ, but also implies the completeness of Christ. Hence, the church is, on the one hand, the fullness of Christ, and on the other hand, the completeness of Christ. In other words, without the church it seems that Christ is not at all complete.

We all must be very careful in understanding this word, for it can stir up vehement arguments in theology. I do not mean that God is incomplete and that He needs man to make Him complete. What I mean is that God in Himself is perfectly complete, but without man He is not complete in the universe according to His plan. Oh, brothers and sisters, this matter is too glorious.

In His eternal plan, God has ordained man to be His vessel, or, in other words, to be His completion. Hence, Genesis chapters one and two show us that when God created man He made two preparations concerning man. The first preparation was that He created man in His image and according to His likeness. As man was created according to God, he resembles God in many aspects. The various aspects of man's expression such as his pleasure, anger, sorrow, joy, preference, choice, etc.—whether it be his emotion, will, or disposition—express God to a certain degree and are miniatures of all that is in God.

Another preparation was that God created for man a spirit in the depths of his being. Of the countless varieties of living things in the universe, only man has a spirit. The angels are spirits, but that is a different matter. In the whole creation there is one kind of created being that is not spirit yet has a spirit, and that is man. Why did God create a spirit for man in the depths of his being? We all know it was because God wants man to receive Him, Who is Spirit. In the same way He created a stomach for man because He wants man to take in food. Consider this: suppose God did not create a stomach for man—how could we take in food? Because we have a stomach, we can receive food into us, enjoy it, digest it, and assimilate it into our being, making it our constituent. In the same manner, since we have a spirit within us, we can receive God into us and assimilate Him, making Him our very constituent.

In the first two chapters of Genesis, when God created man to be His vessel, He made these two steps of preparation: one step was to create man to be like Him, and the other was to put a spirit within man that man might receive Him. After He had made these two preparations He placed Himself before man in the form of the tree of life in order that man might receive Him and obtain Him as life. Brothers and sisters, it is in man's spirit that the contact between God and man is made. Once there is such a contact between God and man, God enters into man to be his content, and man becomes God's vessel to express Him outwardly. Thus God's eternal intention is fulfilled in man.

Please remember, a real prayer is the mutual contact between God and man. Prayer is not just man contacting God, but also God contacting man. If in prayer man does not touch or contact God, and God does not touch or contact man, that prayer is below the proper standard. Every prayer that is up to the standard is one which is a mutual flow and contact between God and man. God and man are just like electric currents flowing into one another. It is hard for you to say that prayer is solely God in man or solely man in God. According to the fact and experience, prayer is the flowing between God and man. Every prayer that is truly up to the standard surely will have a condition of mutual flowing between God and man so that man may actually touch God and God may actually touch man; thus, man is united with God, and God with man. Therefore, the highest and most accurate meaning of prayer is that it is the mutual contact between God and man.

II. PRAYER IS MAN BREATHING GOD, OBTAINING GOD, AND BEING OBTAINED BY GOD

A real prayer is also man breathing in God just as he breathes in air. While you are thus breathing in God, spontaneously you are obtaining God, just as when you breathe in air you receive air. Consequently, not only is God obtained by you and becomes your enjoyment, but also your whole being surrenders to God, turns unto God, and is wholly gained by God. The more you pray, the more you will be filled with God, and the more you will surrender yourself to God and be gained by Him. If you do not pray for a week or, even worse, a month, then you will be quite far from God. What does it mean to be quite far from God? It means that you cannot obtain God and be obtained by Him. The only remedy for this situation is to pray. And it is not enough to pray for only two or three minutes; you must pray again and again until you have actually breathed God and are actually obtained by God, and God by you. Therefore, brothers and sisters, real prayer is of great importance to a Christian's spiritual life.

Brothers and sisters, never think that prayer is merely asking God for something. For example, you need a house and you ask God to prepare one for you. After praying, you receive a word from the Lord saying that what you have asked shall come to pass unto you. The next day a brother comes and says to you, "Do you need a house? My neighbor has two houses for rent; the location is convenient and the rent is cheap." So, you immediately thank and praise the Lord, saying, "Hallelujah, the Lord is really the true and living God; He has answered my prayer." I would not say that this is not prayer, but this is not adequate prayer. Brothers and sisters, if you have really learned the lesson of prayer, whether you can find a house is actually secondary; the primary thing you should be concerned about is whether you have obtained more of God and whether you have been gained more by God through such a prayer. If the result of a prayer is only the accomplishment of a particular matter, without obtaining God or being obtained by God, then such a prayer is a failure, a miscarriage. The ultimate result of a prayer should be that the intercessor gains more of God and is gained more by God, though the thing which he has asked of God may also be fulfilled.

Please consider, are your experiences of prayer like this? Although many times we may not know such a meaning of prayer and may still pray to God concerning certain affairs, God still brings us into Himself through our prayers for those matters. For example, a sister who is a mother loves her child dearly but loves the Lord very little. Regardless how much you help her, she would not seek the Lord. However, one day her child becomes ill. After numerous visits to physicians, the child remains sick. She becomes helpless and has no alternative other than to put her trust in the Lord. When she comes to pray, she only asks the Lord to heal her child. She does not have the slightest intention of seeking the Lord Himself. Who would imagine that through such a prayer she would be able to actually meet Him, touch Him, and enjoy Him? Because of such a prayer, this one, who for many years refused to be gained by the Lord, has spontaneously entered into God and, at the same time, has been gained by God. But still she does not understand what has happened. After three days her child is actually healed, so she comes to the fellowship meeting and testifies how faithful God is, how He has answered her prayer, and how her child has been healed. Although she has obtained the reality in prayer, she still does not realize it. Many times we are just like that ourselves. When we see the desolation of the church and go to the Lord to pray, we feel that we are praying for the church's condition, but in God's view the purpose of our prayer is to cause us to touch Him, inhale Him, obtain Him, and allow Him to obtain us. I believe in the remaining years God will cause every one of His children to become more and more clear that real prayer is not to pray concerning affairs, ask for things, or intercede for people. Real prayer is to inhale God Himself, to obtain God, and to be obtained by God. All those prayers for people, affairs, and things that are outside God are not the essence of prayer but are merely the outer skin or accessories of prayer. A real prayer, a prayer of essence, is one in which you actually contact God, breathe Him, enjoy Him, obtain Him, are filled with Him, and allow Him to gain your being. If the children of God can see this point they will have a better understanding of the real meaning of prayer.

III. PRAYER IS MAN COOPERATING AND CO-WORKING WITH GOD, ALLOWING GOD TO EXPRESS HIMSELF AND HIS DESIRE THROUGH MAN, AND THUS ACCOMPLISH HIS PURPOSE

If a brother or sister has really learned the secret of prayer covered in the preceding two points, spontaneously there will be the following result: such a praying one will certainly cooperate with God, work together with God, and allow God to express Himself and His desire from within him and through him, ultimately accomplishing God's purpose. This is according to Romans 8:26 and 27, which tell us that we do not know for what we should pray as is fitting, but the Holy Spirit intercedes in us according to God's purpose. Actually, we do not know how to pray. We know what people ordinarily call supplication, but we know little about the prayer which is spoken of in the Scriptures. The first time I read these two verses in Romans 8, I questioned their meaning. When I was sick, I thought, did I not pray to God asking him to heal me? When I was in want, did I not pray to God asking Him to send me provision? How could the Scriptures say that we do not know for what we should pray as is fitting? Gradually, the Lord showed me that we really do not know anything about the kind of prayer that God desires. We know those prayers which people generally consider to be prayers but which are below the standard. We do not know those prayers that touch God's desire and are up to the standard. This is our weakness. Thank God, in this matter of our weakness, the Spirit Himself joins in to help us and intercede for us with groanings which cannot be uttered. Brothers, real prayers are the Holy Spirit within man expressing God's desire through man. In other words, real prayers are prayers involving two parties. They are not simply man alone praying to God, but they are the Spirit mingling with man, putting on man, and joining with man in prayer. Outwardly it is man praying, but inwardly it is the Spirit praying. This means two parties express the same prayer at the same time. Please remember that this alone is the prayer which is spoken of in the Scriptures.

We often speak of Elijah's prayer. James 5:17 says, "Elijah was a man subject to like passions as we are, and he prayed earnestly that it might not rain: and it rained not on the earth by the space of three years and six months." "Prayed earnestly" in Greek means prayed with prayer, or prayed in prayer. This is a very peculiar expression in the Bible. Please remember, this is what we mean by prayer of two parties. When Elijah was praying, he was praying with or in a prayer. In other words, he prayed with the prayer of the Spirit within him. Thus we can say that Elijah's prayer was God praying to Himself in Elijah. Andrew Murray once said that a real prayer is Christ Who indwells us praying to Christ Who is sitting on the throne. That Christ would be praying to Christ Himself sounds strange, but in our experience this is really the case.

Let us look again at Romans 8:27. There is a clause which says, "The Spirit...intercedes...according to God." This means that the Holy Spirit prays in us according to God; that is, God prays in us through His Spirit. Thus, such a prayer certainly expresses God's intention as well as God Himself.

By these illustrations we can see that real prayers will certainly cause our being to be wholly mingled with God. We will become a person of two parties, i.e. God mingled with man. When you pray, it is He praying, and when He prays, it is also you praying. When He prays within you, then you express the prayer outwardly. He and you are altogether one, inside and outside; He and you both pray at the same time. At that time you and God cannot be separated, being mingled as one. Consequently, you not only cooperate with God but also work together with God that God Himself and His desire may be expressed through you, thus ultimately accomplishing God's purpose. This is the real prayer which is required of us in the Bible.

Hence, Jude verse 20 says, "Praying in the Holy Spirit." This means you should not pray in yourself. In other words, it means your prayer should be the expression of two parties, you and the Holy Spirit, praying as one. Ephesians 6:18 says, "By means of all prayer and petition, praying at every time in spirit." It is hard to say that the spirit here refers solely to the Holy Spirit. All those who read the Bible from an orthodox viewpoint admit that the spirit here does not refer solely to the Holy Spirit; rather, it also includes our human spirit. When we pray, we must pray in such a mingled spirit.

From our fellowship in this chapter we can see that the Bible is God breathing out Himself, while prayer is our breathing in God. Bible reading and prayer are our breathing before God and thus our breathing in of God. Hence, we should not be those who only read the Bible and fail to pray. If we only read the Word, we do allow God to breathe out Himself, but we still do not breathe in God. Thus, we still need to pray. However, in our prayer our supplications for people, happenings, and things are but the outer skin, the framework. Real prayer always matches the Scriptures; it is an exhaling and inhaling before God, causing us and God, God and us, to contact one another and to obtain one another. Consequently, we wholly cooperate and work with God, and God expresses Himself and His desire through us, ultimately accomplishing His purpose. This is a fundamental meaning of prayer in the Bible.

Chapter Two

THE PRINCIPLES OF PRAYER

Ezekiel 36:37 says, "Thus saith the Lord GOD; I will yet for this be inquired of by the house of Israel, to do it for them; I will increase them with men like a flock."

Jeremiah 29:10-14 says, "For thus saith the LORD, That after seventy years be accomplished at Babylon I will visit you, and perform my good word toward you, in causing you to return to this place. For I know the thoughts that I think toward you, saith the LORD, thoughts of peace, and not of evil, to give you an expected end. Then shall ye call upon me, and ye shall go and pray unto me, and I will hearken unto you. And ye shall seek me, and find me, when ye shall search for me with all your heart. And I will be found of you, saith the LORD: and I will turn away your captivity, and I will gather you from all the nations, and from all the places whither I have driven you, saith the LORD; and I will bring you again into the place whence I caused you to be carried away captive."

We have seen the meaning of prayer; now we come to the principles of prayer. We will point out ten most important principles of prayer. Any good prayer, any prayer of worth, any prayer that is up to the standard, must be in accordance with these principles.

I. PRAYER SHOULD BE INITIATED BY GOD, NOT BY MAN

Concerning the principles of prayer, we must first see that prayer should not be initiated by man but by God. Any prayer, even our confession of sins before God, should be the result of God's working within us. When we pray to confess our sins before God, apparently we are confessing our sins to God according to ourselves, but actually it is God within us initiating such a prayer. Unless the Holy Spirit works within us, we can never go before God to confess our sins. Whenever a person goes before God to confess his sins, it is because the Spirit has initiated this matter in him—urging him, moving him, and causing him to sense his offenses and his need to confess them. In fact, every kind of prayer which we pray should be initiated by the Spirit of God.

If you search through all the experiences of prayer, you will discover that every such experience that can be counted as prayer before God is never initiated by man according to himself, but by the Holy Spirit within man. Any prayer that is started by man on his own is not in accordance with this principle. This is a very serious matter. Unless our prayers are initiated by God from within us, you and I can never have a prayer before God that is acceptable to Him, or prayer that touches His intent and even touches His throne. Thus, strictly speaking, any prayer that is not initiated by God within man, but is merely of man's own initiation, cannot be counted as prayer before God. If we bear this principle in mind, we will be greatly corrected and trained in the matter of prayer.

II. PRAYER IS GOD PASSING THROUGH MAN AND HIS PRAYER

A prayer that measures up to the standard is surely one in which God passes through it. Prayer is not only initiated by God, but God also passes through it. While you are praying, God passes through you and also through your prayer.

This is somewhat like a person speaking in front of a microphone. Electricity passes through the words he speaks. The sound which is heard by those who sit afar has the passing through of the electricity. If he did not use a microphone his speaking would be purely words without the passing through of the electricity. In a sense, it is the same with our prayers. Sometimes it seems that we go before God to pray, but actually it is just we ourselves who are praying—without God passing through. But there are also times we deeply feel that every sentence in our prayer has God in it—God has actually passed through our being. Ordinarily when this condition exists we say that our prayer has touched God, or that it has touched the presence of God. But this does not precisely describe such an experience. It would be more accurate to say that God has passed through our prayer as well as through our being. Brothers and sisters, please review your past experiences. You will see that every prayer you prayed which was of real value before God was one in which God passed through you—God's essence, even God Himself was in your prayer, flowing through your prayer, and also through your being.

III. PRAYER IS MAN AS WELL AS HIS PRAYER PASSING THROUGH GOD

Prayer is not only God passing through us, but every time we prayed an effective prayer which touched God as well as His throne, we also felt that in such prayer we were walking in God, and that even the words of our prayer were spoken in God. Both we, the praying ones, and the words of our prayer passed through God. Because of these two aspects of passing through, when we pray we often sense God's presence more strongly than at any other time. In our daily living, God's presence is with us in the closest, deepest, strongest, and sweetest way when we have had really good prayer. While we pray, on the one hand, it is God passing through our being, and on the other hand, it is also we, our being, passing through God. On one hand, it is God passing through the words of our prayer, while on the other hand, it is the words of our prayer passing through God. Hence, at such a time of prayer we can sense a very strong flavor of God's presence. Let me say this simple word again; prayer is God walking in us, as well as we having our activities in Him. Once we lose such a sense in our prayers, we must immediately adjust ourselves, for we have departed from this particular principle of prayer and have a problem before God.

IV. PRAYER MUST BE GOD AND MAN, MAN AND GOD PRAYING TOGETHER

Prayer is not only a matter of God and man's mutual passing through, but also a matter which God and man do together. I admit that such a saying is seldom heard among Christians. Very few people would tell you that when you pray, you must pray together with God. But in reality, many who pray well have this experience. As we have mentioned in chapter one, a good prayer is Christ in you praying to the Christ on the throne.

I would like to point out one thing. Take the example of one who ministers the Word properly. The words which he speaks are not only his speaking but also the utterance of the Spirit. When such a condition exists, while you are listening you really feel you are touching God. It not only causes you to be stirred, but also, it causes you to touch God. This not only applies to ministering the Word, but also to the matter of prayer. Many times when you pray with the brothers and sisters, such a condition may exist. While someone is praying very properly, you may sense that you have touched God in the words of his prayer and that his utterances are God's coming forth. When we meet this kind of situation we say his spirit has come forth. Actually speaking, it is God coming forth from him, for it is not only he praying there, but God and he praying together. God is praying in him, and he is praying in God. He really can say, "My prayer is God and I; I and God praying together." We have had this kind of experience in the past; however, since it had not been pointed out adequately, there was not the thorough knowledge concerning this matter. Now we can point out from our experience that a prayer which is up to the standard is not only God passing through man and man passing through God, but also man and God, God and man praying together.

V. PRAYER IS NOT FOR MAN HIMSELF BUT FOR GOD

A prayer that is up to the standard must be one in which man is not praying for himself or for others, but for God. Even when we pray for sinners to be saved or for the brothers and sisters to be revived, we ought to be praying for God. In the Bible there are many examples of such prayer. For example, in Daniel chapter nine, Daniel prayed that God would hear and be gracious to Daniel and this people, not for their sake, but for "thine own sake" (v. 19).

Brothers and sisters, what then is prayer? The highest meaning of prayer is that it is a means by which God may gain His authority and benefit. Apparently, you may be praying for many people, for many things, or for yourself, but you must be able to go to the root of the matter and say, "O God, all these prayers are for Your sake. Whether or not my prayers are answered is of very little significance, but Your authority and benefit in these matters are of immense importance. Therefore, although I am praying for these people, events, and matters, actually my prayer is for Your sake. The same is true when I pray for the church. Whether the church is cold or hot, good or bad, dead or living—these are of small concern compared to whether or not Your plan, Your testimony, and Your authority can benefit and gain their rightful places. Therefore, I am not praying for the revival of the church, but for Your authority and benefit." Brothers and sisters, I know for a fact that if we pray in accordance with these first four principles, our prayer will surely be one through which God may gain His authority and benefit. Obviously, if this transpires, the church will be revived.

May the Lord cover me with His blood and allow me to share something from my own experience. There were quite a few times when I suffered want in material things and necessities. The moment I went to pray concerning these things, I was immediately put to the test. As I knelt down before God, there was an asking within, "Are you praying for yourself, or are you praying for God's sake?" Whenever there was such an asking within, I prostrated myself before God and said to Him, "O God, if it were for myself, it would not matter if I suffered poverty and starvation even unto death, but Your authority and benefit are involved. Although I am asking for some material things from You, it is still not for my own sake, but for Your sake. If You would rather let Your authority and benefit suffer loss, my poverty and hunger are insignificant matters." You see, this is a proper prayer.

I know that when some brothers and sisters pray for these necessities, usually they are not so brave and strong. Instead, the moment they kneel down they would shed tears and pray, "O God, have pity on me. I have nothing to eat, I have nothing

to wear, I have no place to live; I beg You, have pity on me."
This kind of prayer is pitiful because it is altogether for yourself. Therefore, in asking God for material things, we may
have two vastly different motives, for God's sake or for ourselves.

Let me ask you, brothers and sisters, what if your child
should get sick today and you go to pray for him. In your
prayer could you say to God, "O God, my child is sick, please
heal him; yet my prayer is not for my own sake, but for Your
sake"? Could you pray such a prayer? Or would you pray feeling your child is so lovely that you wonder what you would do
if he were to die; and therefore, shed tears, earnestly and
mournfully begging God to heal him. If so, I can boldly say
that although your prayer is fervent, it is not in God but
altogether in yourself. Your earnest imploring does not pass
through God nor does it allow God to pass through you; moreover, it is not God and you, you and God, praying together.
Instead, it is purely you yourself praying before God. But
there are some who have learned the lesson and have received
guidance so that when they pray for the healing of their child,
they can also say before God, "O God, this is not for my sake
but for Your sake; this is not my business but Your business.
Not only when this one child is ill, but even if all my children
were sick and all would die, it is Your business, not mine."

Brothers, we must touch this deep and tremendous principle and measure our prayers by it. Then you will discover
even in such a divine matter as prayer, how much you are still
filled with yourself, and how little you have passed through
God's purification. Whether it is in the intention, the motive,
or the expectation of your prayer, there is mixture within you.
Yes, you are praying to God, but in your heart you are praying
wholly on your own and for your own sake. Therefore, you
must be dealt with by God until one day you become able to
say, "O God, I am praying not for myself but for Your sake. In
my motive, intention, and expectation there is no place for
me; rather, everything is for Your sake."

Brothers, if we would learn such a lesson, we would no
longer need to implore God or beg for His pity; instead,
we would be able to pray bravely and strongly, for we would

be praying not for ourselves but for God's sake. I very much like this word which Daniel uttered: "O Lord, hear; O Lord, forgive; O Lord, hearken and do; defer not, for thine own sake" (Dan. 9:19). Without a doubt, Daniel was one who passed through God and allowed God to pass through him. He was also one who prayed with God and allowed God to pray with him. Hence, he could pray, "O Lord, hear...for thine own sake." This is a very basic principle.

VI. PRAYER IS THE EXPRESSION OF GOD'S INTENTION

Every proper prayer is also man speaking forth the intention of God. Yes, it is you who are speaking, but it is God Who is expressing His heart's intent. Your words are the expression of God's intention. For example, you may pray, "O God, forgive me of my sins." This word expresses God's desire to forgive you of your sins. Therefore, true prayers do not express our ideas; rather, they express God's intention through our utterance.

We have said earlier that every prayer which measures up to the standard is not initiated by man but by God. This initiation means that God anoints His intention into man. After man receives this intention, he converts it into words and utters them to God. This is prayer. Therefore, when you pray for the salvation of your relatives and friends, if your prayer is proper, you ought to believe that in the universe God has the intention to save that particular relative or friend of yours. This intention of God could never be expressed or completed by God Himself. This is a law. God desires that all men be saved; this is His intention. But if no one prays for all men, then they cannot be saved. Therefore, unless you pray for your relative or friend and thus express God's desire, His intention cannot be done, and your relative or friend cannot be saved. Hence, when we go before God to pray, we should not immediately pray according to our own ideas, for this kind of prayer is usually initiated by ourselves and not by God. When we pray we must first be quiet before God, fellowship with Him, and allow Him to anoint His intention into us; thus our prayer can express God's intention.

VII. PRAYER IS GOD'S INTENTION ENTERING INTO MAN'S INTENTION

Every proper prayer is also the entering of God's intention into man's intention. A person who prays this way must be one who regularly draws near to God, allows God to gain him, and lives in God, thus affording God the opportunity to put His desire into him. Originally it was God's intention, but now it enters into man and becomes man's inner intent. For example, as mentioned earlier, you may be praying for a certain relative or friend to be saved. While praying you eventually begin to express God's desire to save that particular person. This could only have occurred because you were one who drew near to God. At a certain point, while you were drawing near to God, God put His intention to save that particular relative or friend into you; thus, His desire became your desire. Therefore, when you prayed for this matter, it was as if you were expressing your desire, but actually it was His very desire being expressed.

For this reason, many times when people requested us to pray for them we could not accept their request because we know that proper prayers before God must not be according to our own decision, but according to the burden which we receive from God when we contact Him and touch Him. Hence, at the outset of our praying, we cannot bring others' affairs with us and pray for them.

Because of this, before we open our mouth to pray for some matters, we need to have a considerable length of time to open our being before God. No one who knows how to pray can go before God and immediately open his mouth to pray. Rather, he is one who daily carries with him a spirit of prayer, is silent before God, does not say much, and does not have many suggestions. He prays as God's intentions are anointed into him one by one. Therefore, prayer is also God's intention entering into man's intention.

VIII. PRAYER IS GOD'S HEART'S DESIRE PASSING THROUGH MAN AND RETURNING TO GOD

Every proper prayer is uttered not with words conceived in man's mind but with words issuing from the particular burden within. Where does that burden come from? It comes from the fact that God's intention is being anointed into us through the Spirit and thus becomes our intention. Based upon this intention and burden which we sense within us, we go before God to pray. Therefore, we can say that our prayer is God's intention coming out of God, passing through us, and going back again to Him.

IX. PRAYER IS THE DISCHARGING OF OUR BURDEN BEFORE GOD

In a proper prayer you should always feel very much burdened at the beginning but very light at the end. If at the beginning of your prayer you are indifferent and at the end you are still indifferent; if you are neither burdened nor light; if it seems to make no difference whether you pray or not; then you know your prayer is not up to the standard. A prayer that matches the standard must be one in which you first draw near to God. While you draw near, an intention enters into you which becomes your burden, making you feel the need to go before God to pour out your heart and discharge your burden. Then, after you have prayed adequately, you immediately feel light within; the burden having been discharged. If this condition does not exist, your prayer is not quite proper.

For an illustration, let us use the story of the salvation of Hudson Taylor, founder of the China Inland Mission. His biography tells us that when he was around fifteen or sixteen years old, on the day of his salvation his mother was visiting a relative seventy to eighty miles away. In the afternoon she felt a desperate burden concerning her son's salvation. Hence, she locked herself in a room and prayed before God, pouring out her heart's desire. She prayed until the burden within her was gone, and she felt rather light and free. Then, knowing that God had answered her prayer, she thanked and praised God. While his mother was praying, Hudson Taylor noticed in his father's reading room a gospel tract which contained this word: "the accomplished work of Christ." This simple word touched him and compelled him to receive the Lord as his Savior with his whole heart. After a short while, when his mother came home, Hudson Taylor went to the door to meet her, telling her that he had good news for her. But his mother embraced him with a smile saying, "My son, I already knew some time ago and have been rejoicing over your good news for two weeks."

In this story we can see that, firstly, God's intention was to save Hudson Taylor. At that moment, his mother was looking to the Lord and was quiet before God. Thus, God gained the opportunity to put His intention into the mother, making it her inner burden which she poured out before Him. Ultimately, this burden was completely discharged before the throne of God, and God then came in to bring this prayer to pass.

This illustration should convince us that this prayer not only caused Hudson Taylor to be saved; it also caused the praying mother to enter more deeply into God and to be gained by God in a deeper way. We cannot tell exactly how much the mingling between man and God in her had deepened after that prayer. Moreover, this was not just a matter of a soul being saved. It involved the immeasurably great matters of the authority and benefit which God gained through Hudson Taylor. This should be the result of a proper prayer.

X. THE PURPOSE OF PRAYER IS TO GLORIFY GOD

A proper prayer is not to cause man to have the enjoyment in his accomplishment or in the result, but to cause God to gain one hundred percent of the glory. Yes, it is you who prayed; it is God Who answered your prayer and brought it to pass, but you should not have any place in this. If after a prayer has been fulfilled you have any place in it, then you ought to know there is something wrong with your prayer—you have not as yet thoroughly learned the lessons of prayer. Therefore, this principle is very important.

In Jeremiah 29 God said, "That after seventy years be accomplished at Babylon I will visit you, and perform my good word toward you, in causing you to return to this place. For I know the thoughts that I think toward you, saith the LORD, thoughts of peace, and not of evil, to give you an expected end" (vv. 10-11). These words proclaimed God's intention toward the Israelites; these were things that He intended to do. But, let me ask you, brothers and sisters, how could God carry out His intention? According to God's principle, His intention must be carried out through man's prayer on earth. Without man's prayer, God's desire cannot be fulfilled. What kind of person can be used by God to pray for His intention? There is only one kind, a person who lives before God, waits before Him, and allows God to do the initiating. When you read the book of Daniel you see that Daniel was one who really did not initiate anything before God. He waited before God, caring only for God, not for himself. Thus, he touched and understood this particular intention of God and learned that God would turn again the captivity of the children of Israel after seventy years were accomplished. Since Daniel's desire matched God's intention, he fasted and poured out this desire before God in prayer. Thus God's heart's desire and intention came out from God, went into Daniel, passed through him, and eventually returned to the throne of God. Then the throne of God took immediate action concerning the situation. This action was not at all for Daniel's enjoyment or glorying but for God to gain the glory. This is a very meaningful matter. Although Daniel prayed for others that God would cause them to return, Daniel himself did not go back. He may have returned eventually, but there is no clear record of that in the Bible. It seems that he had asked for one thing and God brought it to pass, yet he himself did not participate in the result.

Therefore, concerning the principles of prayer, your whole being from head to toe must be put aside. Your being does not have much place in prayer. In the beginning it is God who initiates, in the process you are but one who cooperates with God, and ultimately it is for the glory of God. This is real prayer—man being united with God and cooperating with Him on earth, allowing Him to express Himself and accomplish His purpose through man. It is based upon this that we have these ten principles. By the test of these ten principles, you can tell what kind of prayer you are praying. If all these ten principles apply to your prayers, your prayers before God are pure with not much mixture of self in them. But today how few people on earth can pass the test of these ten principles. This requires a very strict learning of the lessons. May God be merciful to us that we may strongly pursue this matter.

Chapter Three

THE MAN OF PRAYER

We know that in whatever we do, the results always depend on the kind of person we are. You may do the same thing someone else does, but when you do it, it turns out another way. The Chinese have this saying: "The outcome of any matter hinges upon the person doing it." Many consider the method the key to everything, but actually the person is more important than the method. The method is dead, but the person is living. Hence, it is not enough just to have a particular method; it is also necessary to have a particular person. And in spiritual matters it can almost be said that the *person* is the *method*. If the person is not right, the method is useless regardless how right it may be; for spiritual things are matters of life, and life does not depend on methods. Life merely expresses itself according to its nature. Thus, regarding spiritual matters, the person equals the method.

In the whole Bible, God seldom taught methods of service to those who served Him; rather, He dealt with the persons themselves. Take the example of Moses, one of the greatest servants of God in the Old Testament. Neither at the time of, nor prior to the time of his calling, is there any record of God telling him many different methods of service. Rather, God spent eighty years dealing with Moses' very being; for in matters of contacting God, the person is the method. Although we have spoken of some principles of prayer which tell us what prayer really is, if our *person* is wrong, and we merely try to pray according to those principles, they will not work. Hence, if we wish to learn how to pray, we must know what kind of person a man of prayer should be. Since this is such an extensive subject, we can only mention some important principles.

I. MUST BE ONE WHO SEEKS GOD AND GOD'S WILL

If a person only knows how to seek after himself and his own desire, he may pray, but he is not a man of prayer. A man of prayer must become such that in all the universe he only cares for God and His will, having no other desire besides this.

We can see this characteristic very clearly in our Lord Jesus when He lived as a man on this earth. When He was praying in Gethsemane, He fellowshipped with God the matter of His death saying, "If it is possible, let this cup pass from Me." But then He also said, "Yet not as I will, but as You will" (Matt. 26:39). Three times He told God, I want Your will, not Mine. Ordinarily we think that when a person prays he asks God to do something for him. For example, he has a desire, so he prays according to his desire and asks God to fulfill it for him. But in Gethsemane we see One Who prayed thus: "Not as I will, but as Thou will." In effect, the Lord Jesus was saying, "Although I am praying here, I am not asking You to accomplish something for Me; rather, I am asking that Your will be done. I seek nothing for Myself in this universe. My only desire is that You may prosper and that Your will may be carried out. I am such a One Who only wants You and Your will."

Again, let us look at the model prayer with which the Lord Jesus taught His disciples how to pray; it is according to the same principle. At the very outset He said, "Let Your name be sanctified; Let Your kingdom come; let Your will be done, as in heaven, so on earth" (Matt. 6:9-10). These words of prayer tell us clearly what His inner desire was. Brothers, if we know only how to pray for our own living, business, and family, then our prayers really fall short. This proves that we are not single and pure before God, but that we are still rather complicated and mixed within—we desire other things besides God.

Sometimes even in God's work we covet something for ourselves. Both our spirit and our heart have not yet been purified to the extent that we only want God and His desire; hence, we are not a man of prayer. We may pray, but as far as our being is concerned, we are not a man of prayer. A man of prayer is one whose many prayers before God are for the sake of His desire—for God to prosper, and for His will to be done. He does not seek his own prosperity, increase, enjoyment, or fulfillment. All he wants is God and God's will; he is satisfied as long as God has a way to go on and accomplish His will. Brothers and sisters, only such a one is a man of prayer.

Although it may seem that this word is a little premature and a little high for a new believer, you and I ought to have the kind of faith that from the start we would cause the new believers to be properly trained concerning prayer. You can tell them simply but clearly that even when we pray concerning the food at breakfast, we should say to God, "O God, although we pray that You give us our daily bread, our prayer is not for our own sake, but for Your sake. We eat and drink because we want to live for You. Even when we pray for such an insignificant matter, our heart is still only for You, not for ourselves. We only want You and Your will, not our enjoyment and prosperity."

Even in doing business, in teaching, and in other things, the principle is the same. You can say to God, "O God, bless this business not for our sake but for Your sake. We are praying here in order that this business may prosper and make some profit, but this is not for ourselves but for Your kingdom."

This same principle also applies to our preaching the gospel and our establishing, administering, and building up the church. Sometimes after suffering a blow in the work one sheds tears sorrowfully before God. But this sorrow may not necessarily be of value and this shedding of tears also may not be remembered by God. God will ask you, "For whom do you feel sorry? And for whom do you shed tears?" God will cause you to see that your inner motive is not pure, but that in God's work you still have your own desire, expectation, and goal.

Therefore, brothers and sisters, whatever we pray for, we must be able to tell God, "O God, I am praying for this matter for Your sake and for Your kingdom's sake—I only care for You and Your will." One who can pray thus is a man of prayer.

Here we must be examined and tried by God. Apparently we are just praying to God for something and asking Him to bring it to pass unto us, but do we realize that our prayers are tests, testing where we stand?

What are we actually after in this universe? What are we for? Do we seek after our own interests or God's? Are we for ourselves or for God? Do we want God to fulfill our desire or His desire? Sooner or later every one of us must be tested in our prayers. Unless one has been led by God to such a state of purity, he is not a man of prayer. He may pray many prayers, but they are of little value before God, and he still cannot be counted as one who works with God, cooperates with Him, prays to Him, and fulfills His will.

II. MUST BE ONE WHO LIVES IN GOD
ALWAYS HAVING FELLOWSHIP WITH HIM

It is not enough that a Christian live before God; he must also learn to live in God. In today's Christianity we often hear people say that we should live before God and have a fearful heart before Him. Of course, these teachings are very good; however, please remember that in the New Testament age it is not enough for man just to live *before* God; it is also necessary that he live *in* God. In John 15:7 the Lord Jesus says, "If you abide in Me and My words abide in you, ask whatever you will, and it shall come to pass to you." In this word the Lord shows us that a man of prayer must be one who abides in Him. To live before the Lord surely is good, but it is quite possible that you and the Lord may still be two; the Lord is the Lord, and you are you. Only when you live in the Lord can you become one with Him. Then you can say to the Lord, "Lord, it is not I alone praying here, but it is You and I, I and You praying together. This is not just I praying before You, but, much more, it is I praying in You. I am one who is united with You and who has become one with You. Thus I can pray in Your name."

The Bible says that we should pray in the name of the Lord. To pray in the name of the Lord is to pray in the Lord. You who pray in the name of the Lord are in the Lord and are a part of Him; you and the Lord have become one. We have often used an illustration to explain the matter of praying in the name of the Lord. Suppose I have some money deposited in the bank, and I write out a check, sign my name on it, and give it to a brother to draw the money from the bank. When he goes to withdraw the money, he represents me, not himself. When the teller releases the money, he does it not according to that brother's name but according to my name. At that moment, that brother is I. The same is true when we pray in the name of the Lord and God answers our prayer. Therefore, in order to be a man of prayer, one must be a man who lives in the Lord.

In John 14, 15, and 16, the Lord Jesus told people to pray in His name. In these three chapters, at least six or seven times the Lord says, "Ask in My name." This is the same as His saying, "Abide in Me," and "You in me, and I in you." To ask in the Lord is to ask in His name. When we pray, it is the Lord praying in us, and we praying in Him; the Lord and we praying together. For we are those who are united with the Lord and have become one with Him.

If you would thus abide in the Lord, there would not be a moment of broken fellowship with the Lord. The flowing of an electric current is the best way to illustrate the fellowship that is spoken of in the Scripture. Spiritual fellowship is a flowing in the spirit—God's Spirit and our spirit, our spirit and God's Spirit—two spirits having mutual fellowship. In a proper prayer, the Spirit of God and the spirit of man always have mutual fellowship, mutual flowing; the two spirits have become one spirit. When we really enter into prayer, we can say, "God, here is a man who lives in You and who has fellowship with You in spirit." Whenever we pray, whether we pray aloud or silently, we must have the sensation that the Spirit of God is moving within us. It is we who are praying, yet it is the Spirit of God moving in us. Such is one who has fellowship with the Lord and who is a man of prayer.

Some say that sufferings will compel us to pray. But I would like to tell you, brothers and sisters, if you have to wait for sufferings to drive you into prayer, then you are not a man of prayer. A proper man of prayer does not wait to pray until sufferings come; rather, he learns to abide in the Lord daily

and have unceasing fellowship with Him. Thus, he spontane-
ously has a spirit of prayer within him. The Holy Spirit is the
Spirit Who grants grace which causes man to beseech God.
Hence, He in man's spirit would surely cause man to pray.

Fellowship with the Lord does not permit any barrier
between you and the Lord. If within you there is a little
thought of unwillingness to forgive others, this unwillingness
to forgive would become a barrier between you and the Lord.
A barrier that is allowed to remain causes you to become
more and more distant from God. It was for this reason that
the Lord said, "Therefore, if you are offering your gift at the
altar and there remember that your brother has anything
against you, leave your gift there before the altar and go
away; first be reconciled to your brother..." (Matt. 5:23-24).
This means that you should not have any problem with
anyone. For once you have a problem with man, there exists a
barrier between you and God, and you cannot be one who
abides in God and who has fellowship with Him.

I think we all have had this kind of experience. Sometimes
it may be because of a certain sin (not necessarily a big one)
which we would not deal with, or a preference or tie which we
would not break off. These immediately become barriers
between us and the Lord. Once we fall into this kind of situation, our spirit of prayer is quenched. This is because we are
not in the Lord, and the fellowship between us and Him is
lost. When the life of prayer is cut off, even if you exercise your mind to conceive a prayer or exercise your will to
squeeze out a prayer, it is futile.

If we just love the world a little and are secretly united to
it, even this would make us unable to pray. Sometimes the
barrier exists because within us there is a little pride, boast-
ing, or showing off. Maybe there is a thought that is not pure
and simple but that desires something for oneself. These are
some factors, or rather, you can call them poisons, which slay
the spirit of prayer within us. If you would be willing to deal
thoroughly with sins, separate yourself completely from
the world, seek simplicity before the Lord, allow the Spirit
of the Lord to purify you, and permit the cross to slay in you
everything that is condemned by the Lord, then you will

immediately see that the spirit of prayer inside you is quickened. You would surely enjoy praying, have the appetite to pray, and be able to pray prevailingly, for at that moment you would be one abiding in the Lord and having fellowship with Him. It is a marvelous thing that the life within us is a life of prayer. If you were to ask me, "What is the primary function of the Holy Spirit within us?" I would say that it is to lead us into prayer. Whenever you yield some room to the Holy Spirit and obey Him a little, the inevitable result is that He leads you to pray. On the other hand, whenever you disobey or quench the Spirit a little, the prayer within you will immediately cease and the spirit of prayer will also disappear. Therefore, brothers and sisters, if you want to be a man of prayer, you must be one who abides in God and one in whom the Spirit of God has room. You must be in the Spirit of God and have continual fellowship with Him, i.e., the two spirits are flowing through one another. The greater the flow, the more prayer you have. You may flow to such an extent that not only can you pray in your room, but the spirit in you can also pray while you are in the car, on the street, or talking with people. Even when you stand up to minister, you can be ministering and still be praying, and when you talk with others and contact them, you can be contacting them and still be praying inside.

The spirit of prayer is a law of prayer, just like the digestion which takes place in the stomach is a law. While I am speaking my stomach is digesting; while I am sleeping it is also digesting; while I am walking it is still digesting. If there is no trouble with my stomach, then its digestive function will continue according to the law in the stomach. In the same principle, in our spirit there is also the law of prayer. Whenever we live in the spirit, allowing the Spirit to have place in us, we will continue in prayer according to the law of prayer in our spirit. At this moment our prayer will be very spontaneous.

Never think that only when one shuts the door and devotes himself to prayer can it be counted as prayer. I admit that this is necessary, but with regard to a man of prayer, the emphasis is not that he should devote himself wholly to prayer; rather, he should allow the spirit of prayer to have room in him. Once the spirit of prayer has place, there is the law of prayer in the spirit causing him to pray at any time; even while he is not outwardly praying, he is still praying.

I hope, therefore, all those who minister the Word will practice this one thing—on the one hand, ministering, and on the other hand, praying. If there is the lust of sin or if anything in our being is reserved for the world, outwardly we may be ministering, yet inwardly there is a blockage. At moments like this, those who listen can tell immediately that our words are outward, empty, dead, and stale, for our words are short of the spirit. But on the other hand, if while we are speaking outwardly, inwardly we are also praying and having fellowship in the spirit; although the words are the same as before, when they go forth, people can sense the freshness. This is a marvelous thing. If one who speaks is living and is in touch with the spirit inwardly, others can sense it. While he is speaking, others can sense that he is not only speaking outwardly, but he is also praying inwardly, touching God, and fellowshipping with Him.

III. MUST BE ONE WHO WAITS
CONSTANTLY BEFORE GOD

A man of prayer is also one who abides in God, waiting wholeheartedly before Him. Everyone who has learned well the lessons of prayer always first waits before God and then slowly gets into prayer. This matter is spoken of in the Psalms where it often says, "Wait thou for God." When you come to pray, you should not hastily open your mouth to express your ideas and to utter your feelings. Rather, you need to stop and put aside your thinking and feeling, so that your whole being will be waiting before God.

There are a number of such examples in the Old Testament. For example, Genesis 18 records the fact that God appeared especially to Abraham and was entertained by Abraham in his tent. On that occasion Abraham served continually before God and asked nothing of Him. God finished the cakes and the calf and spoke the thing concerning Sarah. After He rose up to leave and Abraham walked with Him for a distance, God stopped and said, "Shall I hide from Abraham that thing which I do?" (Gen. 18:17). At that time, God made it clear that He had come to earth in order to judge Sodom. When Abraham heard this, he immediately understood God's desire and knew that He was concerned for Lot, who was in Sodom but who belonged to God. Then Abraham immediately prayed according to God's concern. This shows that he was truly one who waited before God.

This does not mean that we need to shut ourselves in a room all day waiting for God; rather, it means that in our daily living there should be a considerable portion of waiting before God. We do not lightly open our mouth to God, neither do we heedlessly ask God for something. Rather, we always maintain a spirit, an intention, an attitude, and a condition which afford God an opportunity to make us sense His feelings and allow Him to express His own desire in our spirit. We should wait until we touch God's desire and sense His feelings and then pray—this prayer is then initiated by God within us.

I would like to tell you, brothers and sisters, that the first good example of prayer in the Bible is the prayer of Abraham in Genesis 18. Some very important principles are contained in that prayer. When the whole world rejected God, there was a man who wanted God. That man was Abraham. Although apparently he did not live in God, in reality he was one who had fellowship with God and who waited before Him. When he saw God, he did not immediately say, "Jehovah is here, the angels of heaven are here, so I want this, and I want that." No, he did not ask for anything; rather, he waited before God. He waited outside the tent, and after he went with the heavenly visitors for a distance, he still stood and waited before God. It was in this waiting that God had the opportunity to say, "How can I hide from Abraham what I am going to do on earth?" And then He went on to reveal His intention to Abraham.

On that particular occasion God spoke to Abraham in a riddle, not in plain words. Therefore, Abraham's prayer before God was also in a riddle, not in explicit terms. In mentioning Sodom, God's intention was centered on Lot. God wanted someone to pray for Lot so that He might have an opportunity to save him. Abraham knew God's heart, and when he heard God mentioning Sodom, immediately he remembered Lot, who had fallen into Sodom, and began to pray for him before God. The strange thing is this: neither God nor Abraham mentioned the name of Lot. How then do we know that Abraham was praying for Lot? We know because later verses in chapter nineteen tell us that when God razed all the plain and the city of Sodom, He remembered Abraham and saved Lot out of that city. By this we know that both the prayer of Abraham before God and the intercession with which God burdened Abraham were centered upon Lot. Neither God nor Abraham mentioned Lot's name, yet both God's heart and Abraham's heart were set on Lot.

Abraham was able to have such a prayer that touched God's heart because he was one who waited before God. He did not have many opinions, supplications, requests, and suggestions; he was one who ceased the activity of his own being before God. He waited before God, affording Him the opportunity to speak, then prayed according to what God said. A man of prayer, therefore, is definitely one who can wait before God. This is a very deep lesson which we need to learn thoroughly. A man going before God to pray must cease his being. That is, his emotion, mind, and will must be halted to a considerable extent. Only such a one who halts the activity of his own being can wait before God.

IV. MUST BE ONE WHO PUTS EVERYTHING OF HIMSELF ASIDE, ESPECIALLY HIS ABILITY AND OPINIONS

One who learns to pray must learn the strict lesson of putting himself aside and halting his being. The self here refers especially to self-opinions and natural ability. In Acts 10 there was a man, Peter, who went up on the housetop to pray. At that time, he had already passed through Pentecost and had a considerable amount of spiritual experience, yet his prayer shows that he still could not put aside his own opinion. Although he went up on the housetop to pray, he still argued with God there and needed God to give him the vision once again. When he saw a great sheet descending from heaven and heard a voice saying, "Rise, Peter; kill, and eat," he said, "Not so, Lord; for I have never eaten any thing that is common or unclean" (Acts 10:13-14). This was his opinion. God spoke to him immediately, "What God hath cleansed, that call not thou common" (Acts 10:15). Here Peter's opinion conflicted with God's will; therefore, he could not get through in his prayer.

Never think that in the matter of prayer we have fewer conflicts with God than Peter had. When we come before God, we have too many opinions. Please read the many prayers in the Bible. You can see man's natural ability as well as human opinions in a good number of them. Jonah is a good example in the Old Testament. When he was praying, he could not put his opinion aside. He prayed his opinion, which was in conflict with God. Again, look at Peter. On the night the Lord Jesus was betrayed, it seemed that he was praying to the Lord, saying, "Although all shall be caused to stumble, yet I will not, even if I must die with You." As Peter was holding very tightly to his natural ability, the Lord could not answer his prayer. His prayer was: "Even if others were caused to stumble, I still would ask You to make me stand firmly." Although he did not state it in this way, you must believe that he hoped to be able to stand. That hope was his desire before God. But the Lord said, "You will surely fall; I cannot answer your prayer to bring success to your natural ability."

One who prays before God should be one who always falls down before God. The strongest illustration of this is Jacob's experience at the ford of Jabbok. At that time, his prayer before God was really full of his natural strength. There he even wrestled with God to the extent that God, having no alternative, was compelled to touch the hollow of his thigh. As a result, Jacob became a cripple. There are numerous such examples in the Scripture. A good number of men went before God and prayed by their natural strength and according to their own opinions—both of which are the greatest hindrances to prayer.

Therefore, a true man of prayer is surely one who falls down before God, and whose natural strength as well as opinions and views have been broken by God. In both the Old

Testament and the New Testament, all who were able to touch God and pray before Him were those whose natural strength had gone bankrupt and whose own views had been laid aside. Daniel was one who completely fell down before God—he had neither his strength nor his views. The same is true with David, in the Psalms. Hence all proper men of prayer are very soft before God. They have put self aside, have fallen down before God, and have been broken. They do not have their insistence, natural strength, ideas and opinions. Only such men can touch God's throne and His will as well. Only such men can be men of prayer.

V. MUST BE ONE WHO IS WILLING TO PAY ANY PRICE TO YIELD TO ALL GOD'S DEMANDS

Another requirement of a man of prayer is that he must be willing to pay any price to yield to God's every demand. I would like to tell the children of God that there cannot be a single instance in which you meet God in fellowship that He does not demand anything from you. Every time you meet Him, He demands something from you. We always think that God is a God Who bestows grace upon us. But I would like to tell you, brothers and sisters, God is also a God Who makes demands upon us.

I am afraid that it has never occurred to some of the brothers and sisters that God is a God of demands. It cannot be denied that God gives us supply, but we all must remember that we do not need to pray for God's supply, for all His supply is ours already. What we need the most is God's stripping. Although the cross is a plus sign, actually it is a minus sign. Our problem today is not that we have too few things upon us; rather, we have too many things in us. Thus, whenever God meets us He demands that we get rid of something.

Please read the story of Abraham. From the beginning when he was met by God until he finally came to know God, there was not a single time God appeared to him that He did not strip him of something. The first time God said, "Get thee out of thy country, and from thy kindred," the second time He said, "Get thee out from thy father's house" (Gen. 12:1). The first time was to strip him of his country; the second time was to strip him of his father. At another time he was stripped of Lot. Abraham proceeded on his way, dragging Lot, whom he should have left behind; for Lot was of his country, kindred, and father's house. Then, in chapter fifteen, when he eventually let go of Lot, he turned his dependence to Eliezer of Damascus. He told God, "Lord God...the steward of my house is this Eliezer of Damascus..." (Gen. 15:2). But God said, no, "This shall not be thine heir..." (Gen. 15:4). Even this one had to be dropped. Later, in chapter sixteen, he acquired Hagar and begat Ishmael. More and more were added to him, but these acquisitions were given to him by Egypt and not by the cross. Therefore, in chapter seventeen, God came to him saying, "You need to be circumcised and get rid of something, for you have too many things in you." The covenant which God made with Abraham was a covenant of decreasing and not of increasing. Then, in chapter twenty-one, God said formally that both Hagar and Ishmael needed to be cast out. I tell you, even the very last one that remained, Isaac, who was a work of God's grace, had to be offered up. We say that Abraham was one who inherited the blessings, yet when we read the stories of his dealings with God we seldom see him receiving anything from God; rather, what we see over and over again are God's strippings and His making demands upon him.

There is one thing I can tell the children of God with full assurance: if God has not demanded something of you today, then you have not met Him today. Every time you encounter God He will demand something of you. If your prayer touches God, you encounter a demand. Therefore, you must be ready to pay the price. Not only that which is born of the flesh needs to be gotten rid of, even that which is gained through grace also needs to be stripped off. Ishmael needs to be cast out, and Isaac needs to be offered up. Every true prayer will cause you to touch God, and every one who touches God encounters His demands. Hence, a man of prayer is definitely one who pays the price.

Brothers and sisters, our problem before God is not that we lack something but that we have excess. Our problem lies not in our deficiency but in our sufficiency. We have so many things in us that every time God touches us something has to go. Because God makes demands every time, we need to pay the price every time. If God has a demand, but you would not satisfy Him by paying the price of meeting that demand, then it would be very hard to maintain a free, flowing fellowship between you and Him, and you would not be able to live in the Spirit of prayer. Although you still could pray, you would not be a man of prayer. Therefore, in order to be a man of prayer, one needs to be willing to pay the price. Whatever God demands of you, you can say, "God, by Your grace I am willing to pay this price. Even if it be Isaac whom You gave to me, if You so desire, I am willing to send him to the altar." He who is willing to thus pay the price to satisfy God's desire is a man of prayer.

VI. MUST BE ONE WHOSE LIVING CORRESPONDS TO HIS PRAYER

As a man of prayer, your living must be consistent, or must correspond, to what you pray. Someone may be asking the Lord for the revival of the church or the salvation of a sinner, yet his living is utterly inconsistent with his prayer. He does not live a life that contributes to the revival of the church, nor does he live in a condition that is conducive to bringing sinners to salvation. Although he may be praying, he is not a man of prayer. A man of prayer not only performs the action of prayer but also lives the life of prayer—his living is prayer. Many times we pray for a number of things, but, after praying, we do not live according to the standard of life required by those things. This means we go through the motions of prayer, but we are not men of prayer.

Therefore, brothers, please remember, inwardly speaking, prayer is our life, and outwardly speaking, prayer is our living. Prayer is neither a thing nor a work. Of course, in a sense, prayer is a work, but your being must be in the prayer and even must be the prayer. For example, a brother may pray asking God to revive the church. While he was asking God to revive the church, his words were altogether in earnest: his tears came down, and you, praying there with him, could really sense his seriousness and also feel that he was fully burdened. Yet, unexpectedly, after the prayer he rose and went to watch a movie. Do you think he is a man of prayer? Of course, I do not mean that after praying we all need to pretend by having a gloomy and sad countenance; the Lord Jesus told us that we should not do that. When you fast and pray you still need to anoint your head—it is useless to pretend. The point is this: real prayer has a condition; that is, if you want to have real prayers, your living should be in accordance with those prayers. There is no way for anyone to believe that your heart is really bearing the burden of the church if, as soon as prayer is over, you can go to watch a movie. Your living does not correspond to your prayer. If you are a man of prayer, your living will definitely be absolutely one with your prayer. Your living is your prayer. The life within is a life of prayer, and the living without is a living of prayer; thus you are a man of prayer.

Some may tell you that prayer needs faith. But faith is not something you can have just because you want it. Actually speaking, faith is a function that emanates from God within us. If you are one who abides in God, lives in Him, and allows Him to have standing in you, then God in you issues forth a function which is faith. Faith does not come from you. We can almost say that faith is God Himself, just like power is God Himself. Only when a person is filled with God is he filled with power. Likewise, only a person who is filled with God is full of faith. It is useless, therefore, to merely exhort people to have faith. If I preach a hundred messages telling you that you need to have faith, you still will not have faith. If you really want to have faith, you need to be a man of prayer who lives in God, is being dealt with by Him, is willing to yield to His demands, and who gives permission to His strippings. When He thus has place in you, then He is the faith in you. When He fills you with Himself, you are full of faith. You do not need to strive to believe nor compel yourself to believe, but you surely can believe. For within you there is a God to Whom you pray, and He is the very God Who fills you and moves you to pray—He has become your faith. Please remember, at this time, you know with assurance that your prayer is acceptable to Him, is of Him, is touching Him, and therefore

He cannot help but answer your prayer. This is faith. Faith does not come according to your wish. Rather, it is God in you filling you to such an extent that you cannot help but have faith. May the brothers and sisters not only learn how to pray, but by the grace of the Lord, be men of prayer.

CHAPTER FOUR

THE LIFE OF PRAYER

In whatever we do, we need the life that corresponds to the accomplishment of that thing. It is a fact that only a particular life can do a particular thing. Prayer is no exception to that rule. Prayer is a matter that is extremely spiritual, holy, and transcendent; hence, it requires a particular life even more than other things do. In order to pray properly, we should not only pay attention to the outward behavior, but we should go deeper to know the inward life of prayer. When I was young, I read several books about prayer and received some help at that time. Gradually, as I advanced a few steps in the Lord, I realized the help was rather superficial and without much weight. More and more, I have come to know that prayer is not a matter of outward behavior, but is altogether something inward. Therefore, we must know the conditions necessary for proper prayer. We saw in chapter three that the man must be proper and right before God. There is also the need to pay attention to the inward condition of the man, that is, the life of prayer within that man.

I. THIS LIFE IS THE LIFE OF GOD WITHIN US

After we have been saved, we have God living in us to be our life. This life is the life of prayer within us. The first function, the characteristic and the ability of this life, is to pray. Therefore, after being saved, the thing a proper Christian likes to do most is pray. For example, characteristically, a duck likes to swim in the water. If you send a little chicken and a little duck to the water, the chicken will run away hurriedly, while the little duck will quickly go in to swim. This happens because the characteristic of the love of water is in the duck's nature. Similarly, the life of God within us has a characteristic that loves to pray. All real believers are like this. If they stop praying for three days, they do not feel good inside. If they stop praying for one week, they will feel even worse within. If they stop praying for a long while they will feel as if they have lost something or some dear ones have died. On the contrary, whenever they pray they feel good inside, because a characteristic of the life within them is that it likes to pray. It not only demands prayer, but it also has the ability to pray.

Actually, we cannot teach a person to pray. The most we can do is point out a way, for the real ability to pray is hidden in the life of a Christian. As long as you are a saved one, there is such a life with such a function within you. Yes, we do teach the brothers and sisters to pray; but please remember, we can only teach because within them there is already a life with such a function. For example, you cannot teach a dog to speak. No matter how hard you try it is futile, for within the dog there is no ability to speak. This ability is not found in the animal life, but only in the human life. If I am always conversing with an Englishman, I believe after five or six months I will be able to speak English very fluently. However, we may have cats and dogs in our homes that have been with us for years yet cannot speak one sentence because they do not have that ability within them. In like manner, no matter how hard you try to teach an unsaved person to pray, he still cannot pray, does not like to pray, and is bothered whenever he sees Christians praying. In fact, some friends told me that whenever they saw us kneeling down to pray, they felt quite embarrassed. They do not understand that we would have felt uneasy unless we did pray. The God Whom we have received has become our life within, and this life has a function; that function is to pray. As long as we do not restrict this life, but give it the liberty and the opportunity to be exercised, then not only does it desire to pray, it will pray.

Of course, just as man needs training for speech, he also needs training for proper prayer. Prayers will improve more rapidly with some guidance, but this is altogether a different matter. We need to see that it is God's life within us that becomes our life of prayer. Therefore, if we desire to be a man of prayer, we must learn to always live in God. The more we live in God, the more the characteristic of this life will be manifested, and the more we will desire to pray. This life within us has a characteristic that makes us desire to pray, an ability that enables us to pray, and a demand that requires us to live in God. Therefore, prayer is a matter of life.

In helping new believers, we need to point out strongly that prayer is not just an outward activity but an inward matter of life. Prayer issues from the characteristics and abilities of a life, and this life is the very life of God. Hence, God requires you to always live in His life. Whenever the fellowship between you and God is interrupted, this life in you is in a half-dead state; consequently, you dislike praying and you are almost unable to pray. You must restore the fellowship with God and live in Him, thus causing the life within you to be resurrected. Thus, spontaneously you can touch the consciousness of prayer within, you have the desire and interest to pray, and you possess the ability to pray. You know what to say and how to say it, and you also know which word of prayer can touch God's throne and hit the center of His heart. Others may not be able to teach you, but you know inside because this is a matter of the inward life. The life in you has the ability to enable you to pray. Of course, if you always pray with those who pray properly, you will automatically follow their manner of prayer. In the same respect, if you are always with Northerners, you will speak with a northern accent; but if you stay with Southerners for a long time, you will then speak with a southern accent. This is unavoidable.

II. THIS LIFE IS HOLY, SEPARATED

This prayer life within us, because it is the life of God, is separated from everything that is unbecoming to God. This life, therefore, requires you to be separated from the world, and demands that you put aside anything that is outside God. If you want to be a man of prayer who can pray, is willing to pray, and who prays properly, you must agree with the demand of the life in you by putting aside whatever it wants you to put aside. Whenever you disagree even slightly with its demand for holiness, you put to death the life of prayer. It is as if you have seized it by the throat. Never think to yourself, "Oh, it is just a little worldliness; it is not a great sin." It is not a matter of great or small, but whether or not this life makes a demand in you. If it demands of you to forsake something that is outside God, then you should do it.

Brothers and sisters, I believe that you have had this kind of experience. Sometimes this holy life within you demands that you not wear a certain dress. When it makes such a demand, you may reason and say, "This is not sinful, and it does not matter if I wear it." You may reason, but the life of prayer would not listen to you. Once the life of prayer within you makes a demand for holiness, it never listens to any argument. If you do not agree, you cannot pray afterwards.

Why is it that today, when the brothers and sisters come together, they often cannot open their mouths? It is because we all have some problems in agreeing with the demands of holiness within us. Many times the brothers and sisters, even though you encourage them, cannot open their mouths in the meeting. This is because they have rejected the demands of holiness in them. Demands of holiness do not come from doctrines but wholly from the life of prayer within.

Therefore, if we want to learn the lesson of prayer, we must pay heed to whatever the life of prayer within demands of us. I repeat, what this life within demands of us is holiness. It requires that we be separated from all people, activities, and things that are outside God. One thing is certain: the more you pray to God by this life, the more stringent the demands of this life within you become. If you always live in this life of prayer, you do not need much outward teaching on the part of men. The more you pray, the more this life in you is being exercised, and the more its function of separating becomes manifest.

No one can be holier than one who continually prays before God. The most holy person is one who constantly prays before God. When he prays, the life in him becomes exercised and spontaneously brings forth the sanctifying function. It demands that he separate himself from this activity and that activity, and when he prays again, it further requires him to put aside this thing and that thing. As he prays still more, it further demands of him to leave this person and that person. The more he yields to the sanctifying demands, the more living the life of prayer in him becomes, and spontaneously he has a greater appetite for prayer. Furthermore, the more his ability to pray increases, the more his praises, thanksgivings, supplications, expressions, and even his utterance are special. Now his technique of prayer greatly excels what it was before. All these conditions prove that he has been continually yielding to the demands of holiness which were made by the life of prayer within him.

For example, many like to go to the movies. This is like a bug which pesters God's children. It is very hard to get rid of, because, unconsciously, it comes back again and again. Brothers and sisters who go to the movies would have to admit that they cannot pray while watching the movies or after they come home from the movies. They cannot pray because they have not yielded themselves to the demand of holiness. While they were yet intending, desiring, and planning to go to the movie, the life of prayer within them had already demanded that they not go. Nevertheless, they still hardened their hearts saying, "We don't care; we are going to see the movie even if it causes us to be in darkness. After this movie, we will get in fellowship with the Lord again." Thus, while walking toward the theater, inwardly something was bothering them. After they came home from the movie they could not pray for a long while. Why is this so? The sole reason is that they had rejected the demands of holiness within and thus hurt the life of prayer.

On the contrary, let us consider someone else who, after being saved, also desired to see a movie. However, while he was going on his way to the movie, he felt rather uneasy and immediately was willing to care for this uneasy feeling. Agreeing with this demand of sanctification, he would say to the Lord, "Lord, I am not going anymore, and I abandon this matter by trusting You." Immediately, in him there would be the desire to pray. He could pray for the church, his relatives, and friends. He would have the burden of prayer in him instantly.

Therefore, we must clearly see that the life of God in every man of prayer is holy and separated. It rejects anything that does not correspond with the divine nature. This life requires that he be fitted wholly with the nature of God. It neither argues nor listens to arguments. If one does not take care of the requirement of the life of prayer within him, he puts it to death and cannot pray. On the contrary, the moment he agrees with its demands, the life of prayer is immediately quickened.

III. THIS LIFE ABSOLUTELY HATES SINS

Since the life of prayer within us is also a life that hates sins, one who wishes to learn how to pray must also thoroughly deal with sins. This life within man has a characteristic that hates sins and also an ability that enables man to deal with sins. If you are even slightly defiled by sins, or love the world a little, immediately there is the consciousness within that you do not correspond to the characteristic of this life. Not only sins and the world, but even a little pride, criticism, despising others, introspection, self-boasting, or presumptuous thought will make you unable to pray. Any dishonesty, unfaithfulness, unrighteousness, or injustice will quench the life of prayer.

There is nothing that causes a man to be dealt with before God more severely than prayer. A proper man of prayer is always being dealt with before God when he prays. Some have learned such a strict lesson that often out of twenty minutes of prayer, fifteen minutes are spent being dealt with by God, while only the remaining five minutes are used to ask something of God. Unfortunately, others are not like this. They always ignore the demands and the condemnations of the life within. They go before God in a very light way and, without being dealt with, immediately open their mouth to pray. Such prayer is just beating the air, is unreal, and is not readily answered by God.

If you do not deal with sins properly, they will create a distance between you and God. The more the sins, the greater the distance will be, making you unable to pray to

God. Therefore, in order to eliminate the distance, you need to first deal with sins. In your prayer you need to confess your sins one by one according to the inner consciousness of life. With each confession you make, you advance one step. After you have confessed all your sins thoroughly, the distance is gone, and when you open your mouth to pray, you will definitely be able to touch God. Your words are not beating the air; rather, every word is able to touch God.

Herein the faith of prayer also issues forth. Whenever you go before God to pray, the life in you hates sins and has the consciousness of them. You must confess your sins one by one according to what it condemns. Then this life releases you within and justifies you. Now you are one who is before God, having no distance or barrier between you and Him. At this time, as there is neither condemnation nor a leak in your conscience, every word penetrates to God. After such prayer, spontaneously you have the assurance, and you are able to believe that God has heard your prayer.

If you allow your sins to remain and you pray without dealing with them, there will surely be a distance between you and God, and your conscience will definitely condemn you. If there is a hole or a leak in your conscience, it is difficult to have faith after you pray. If one's conscience has a hole, his faith will leak out. In other words, one whose conscience is impure and has a leak cannot easily have faith. Though he may pray, he does not have the assurance, for his prayer does not lay hold of God. Please remember, to have the assurance that your prayer touches God, you must deal with your sins according to the demands issuing from the sin-hating nature that is within you. This is a great principle in the Bible.

Consider the story of the Samaritan woman in John, chapter four. When she found that the Lord Jesus had living water to quench her thirst, she asked of Him immediately, saying, "Sir, give me this water." She wanted the living water. But the Lord Jesus replied by touching the matter of her sins. The Lord said, "Go, call your husband, and come here." Whenever we go before God to pray, the Lord touches the matter of our sins. Also, He will touch whatever failings we have in our intentions, motives, actions, or attitudes.

Brothers and sisters, when the Lord touches our failings, are we willing to receive His correction? This is a big problem. Take for example, a brother who has obviously offended his wife. When he prays, the sin-hating life gives him a feeling that he must not only confess his sin before God, but also ask forgiveness from his wife. Being a proud man, he would not ask forgiveness from his wife and consequently, because of his unwillingness to deal with this matter, he would not be able to pray anymore. This continues for a long period of time, until one day God so compels him that he has to go before his wife and bow his head, saying, "I was wrong in that matter on that day, please forgive me." Wondrously, when he thus confesses, the life in him immediately releases him and he is able to pray again.

Here is another example. Suppose that during the Lord's table meeting you become disgusted with a brother's prayer, and because of your disgust, when you go home you cannot pray. In order for you to pray, you have to first confess this sin. At that time, you have to go according to the sense of condemnation in you and say to the Lord, "O Lord, at the Lord's table I despised that brother's prayer. Do forgive me." You must confess your sin or you cannot pray, and you will always feel that there is a distance between you and God. Unless you confess your sins, your prayers cannot touch God. All these principles are related to the life within us.

Therefore, the best way to cause a man to hate sins, condemn sins, reject sins, and stay far away from sins is for him to come before God in prayer. If you have not prayed even once in three days, it is useless to reckon yourself dead daily; the sins are still upon you and you cannot overcome them. But if you regularly go before God to pray and to deal with sins according to the inner sense of life, eventually you will be free from your sins, your inner being will be quickened, and you will love to pray and will be able to pray, for the life of prayer is a life that hates sins.

IV. THIS LIFE LOVES LIGHT

We know that crookedness and craftiness are elements of darkness; while goodness, righteousness, truthfulness, and uprightness are characteristics of light. We are surely in darkness if there is crookedness or craftiness in our motive, manner of life, action, and conversation. Sometimes these conditions are absent, yet there is another kind of darkness, which is pure darkness. Some are in darkness because of crookedness, craftiness, or pride; others are in darkness by simply being dark inside and without light. It may be that one is a very well-behaved person, not a bit crafty, but upright, sincere, guileless, unpretentious, and humble. He has no faults whatsoever, but he is dark within, being void of light. Please remember, any form of darkness can make you unable to pray. Man cannot pray as long as he is dark inside.

You may consider, "It is true that craftiness, crookedness, and pride can cause us to be dark inside, but how can we be in darkness when there is no fault whatsoever?" All darkness is due to some problem, but there can be a kind of darkness even when there is no moral fault. In reality spiritually speaking, this kind of darkness has some underlying problem too. Why is there darkness in man? It is mainly because man remains closed and veiled within. Sometimes you meet a brother or sister who is well-behaved, humble, and loving, but his being is not open. He is neither open to God nor to fellow members of the Body. He is closed to God as well as to man. Not only so, he is also one who evidently rejects light. When light illumines him, he pays no attention to it and even uses an excuse to reject it. Consequently, as he is closed and refuses light, he is a good person yet remains in darkness.

One thing is sure, whatever kind of darkness he may be in, it will always cause man to become unable to pray. The crooked or proud ones will surely dislike praying. The subtle ones and man-haters definitely cannot pray. Similarly, one who is closed to God as well as to man, and who refuses light, certainly will not enjoy praying. For the life of prayer in us is a life that loves light. The more we open ourselves to God as well as to all the brothers and sisters, the more we receive light and allow it to correct us. When we thus remain in the light, within us there will be an intense desire to pray.

I have met some brothers and sisters who are truly humble, meek, loving, sincere, and upright, yet they simply do not like to pray. They enjoy running some errands as well as exerting their effort to perform some things for you, but if you mention prayer to them, immediately they dislike it. They are really lovable, but unfortunately, they do not like to pray. Once you encounter this kind of situation, you should know that they are people who remain in darkness. Their darkness is not due to pride, craftiness, crookedness, or hatred; rather, it is because they do not open themselves, they refuse light, and use excuses to push light away. Hence, they dislike praying. The life of prayer in us loves light, and the more we are in the light, the more the life in us loves to pray—this is a law.

V. THIS LIFE HAS AN INHERENT LAW OF PRAYER

Within every kind of life there are many laws. Such is the case with our physical life. Digestion is a law, and metabolism is another law. What is a law? A law is a natural ability which does not require you to control it by exercising your will. For example, when we take in food, the stomach will spontaneously digest it. This is the law of digestion. Without any help, some elements will automatically be discharged from our body, while other elements will be added into us. This is the law of metabolism. When you wave an object in front of someone's eyes, his eyes will naturally blink. This is also a law. When you eat something bitter, you immediately spit it out; when you taste something sweet, you swallow it. These are laws. Similarly, in our life of prayer there is also a law of prayer. It contains such a natural ability that without your urging, it spontaneously desires to pray.

Remember, however, that although it is a law, it can be damaged by man just as the law of digestion and the law of metabolism can be spoiled by man. We all know that when any physical law is damaged, the result is sickness. Whenever the body is sick, it means its law or laws have been violated. Likewise, if you do not respond to the demand of holiness which issues out of the life within you, this is a sickness which frustrates the law of prayer. If you do not deal with sins according to the consciousness of life, or if you refuse to depart from darkness, this will also obstruct the law of prayer. In other words, it means you are sick. Therefore, with those brothers and sisters who seldom open their mouths to pray, without doubt they are sick in their life of prayer. If you learn to live in God, respond to His demand of holiness, follow the sense of His condemnation, and deal with any darkness, you will discover that the life of prayer in you is healthy and normal, and the law of prayer operates in you continually. Thus, spontaneously, you can pray as well as enjoy praying.

Within every man there is the law of digestion which automatically digests the food that has been taken in. If one does not take in food when it is time to eat, there will be a sensation of emptiness and hunger. If you feel no hunger after not eating for two days, the law of digestion in you has probably been damaged. There is also a law of prayer that is inherent in the life of a Christian which requires you to pray regularly. What kind of people cannot pray? It must be those in whom the law of prayer has been damaged. It may be that they do not respond to the demand of holiness, follow the consciousness of holiness within, or refuse the darkness which is abhorred by the life within. This life is absolutely holy; therefore, it demands that you be holy. It also utterly hates sins; hence, it repeatedly gives you the sense of hating sins. Moreover, it fully loves light, so it always requires you to leave darkness. If you are not willing to respond to its demand of holiness, if you neglect its sin-hating consciousness, or reject its demand of light, your life of prayer is in trouble immediately. If you are willing to deal with these things, the life of prayer within you is immediately resurrected. Moreover, there is a law in this life that will operate in you and make you pray. You will be able to pray as well as enjoy praying, and whatever you pray will touch God. These are abilities inherent in the life of prayer.

CHAPTER FIVE

THE SPIRIT OF PRAYER

Scripture reading:

John 4:24: "God is Spirit; and those who worship Him must worship in spirit and reality."

Jude 20: "praying in the Holy Spirit."

Ephesians 6:18: "praying...in spirit..."

Romans 8:26: "the Spirit Himself intercedes for us..."

I. PRAYER MUST BE IN SPIRIT

We know that the existence and operation of the universe and everything in it is governed by laws. If we want to do anything effectively we must keep the particular laws of that thing. Concerning prayer, there is an iron-clad law: prayer must be in spirit; for in praying you pray to God, and God is Spirit. If you pray in the mind, emotion, or will, but not in spirit, you cannot touch God nor pray *into* Him. These faculties cannot get you through to Him. In order to touch God and pray *into* Him, we must pray in spirit. It is when the Holy Spirit utters prayers in and with our spirit that we can touch God.

Even a sinner who repents and prays to the Lord after hearing the gospel must pray from his spirit in order to touch God and be saved. Until that time he is not yet regenerated, and his spirit is still not quickened; but when the Holy Spirit moves him, enlightens his conscience, and causes him to repent, he prays from his enlightened conscience. Since the conscience constitutes a major part of the spirit, a prayer that comes out from the conscience is a prayer that comes out from the spirit. Having been enlightened by God as well as touched by the Holy Spirit, the conscience is convicted of sin. The cry that issues from such a condemning conscience is, no doubt, a prayer in spirit. Hence, such prayer can contact God, and there is an echo within us. However, there are some who pray when they first hear the gospel, yet there is no response. They have heard some doctrine, received some instruction mentally, and have made a confession before God according to their mind, but their conscience remained untouched. Such prayer cannot touch God.

As the children of God who have been regenerated and have the Holy Spirit dwelling within, our prayers must be in spirit to touch God and be answered. This is the first point about which we should be clear.

II. PRAYER REQUIRES THE EXERCISING OF THE SPIRIT

Since prayer should be in spirit, it requires the exercising of the spirit. One who never exercises his spirit does not know how to pray. For example, a runner must exercise his legs in order to run. A boxer exercises to concentrate the strength of his whole being into his fists. Those learning a language must train their tongue if they would speak that language. Learning to speak Mandarin is difficult because of the sounds which require rolling the tongue. This is difficult not only for foreigners, but also for those from the southern regions of China. Therefore, whatever we do, we need to train the faculty involved.

Likewise, if we want to pray, we must exercise our spirit. If someone cannot pray well and is not willing to pray, it must be because his praying faculty lacks exercise. Whenever an organ lacks exercise it ceases to function properly. Medical doctors tell us that if we cover the eyes from light for three years, when the cover is removed the eyes will not be able to see anything. Although the rest of the body may be strong, the eyes will have lost their function after such a long period of non-exercise. One time an illness forced me to take complete bed rest for six continuous months. After I recovered, I got out of bed and, to my surprise, fell to the floor. I found myself unable to stand or walk. I then realized that since my legs and feet had not been used for six months, they had lost the ability to stand. Therefore, I had to learn how to stand, and then, after a long period of exercise, I was able to walk again. Although you have the legs and feet, the organs for walking, they are useless unless they have been exercised. Similarly, the spirit is the organ for praying. In order to pray we need to exercise the spirit. Never consider that since we have a spirit, then surely we can pray competently. The fact is, unless our spirit has gone through some exercise we cannot pray and we will not enjoy praying. The less we practice something, the less we enjoy doing it, and the less we are able to do it.

Thus, if someone does not pray regularly and you ask him to pray, it is really a hardship for him. It is not because he has a lazy disposition; rather, it is that his spirit is lazy. To people who cannot walk well it is a real suffering if you compel them to walk. On the other hand, those who really enjoy walking will eagerly accept an invitation to walk somewhere. This is because their legs are very strong and agile from exercise. Some brothers and sisters have a spirit of prayer that is very strong and agile. Before you finish mentioning a matter, such a person will have begun to pray in his spirit. But there are some whose spirit of prayer is very lazy because they do not ordinarily use their spirit. Some are very strong-willed, so that when they encounter something it is not their spirit but their will that comes first. Others are very emotional, so that when something happens their emotion takes the lead. With others who are sober-minded and very quick to think, their mind takes the lead in any situation. But all who learn how to pray must exercise themselves to let the spirit dominate in every situation and not allow their mind, will, or emotion to take the lead. We need to train ourselves so that whenever we encounter some problem we can exercise our spirit immediately.

Some have heard the teaching concerning the exercise of the spirit, but since, in reality, they do not practice it much, their spirit is still weak. Such a person especially has difficulty exercising his spirit in prayer. Just as when I lay on the bed for six months my legs became the weakest parts of my whole being, when one does not exercise his spirit it becomes the weakest part of his whole being. My weight increased, and my blood count improved, but due to lack of exercise the walking ability of my legs decreased. Due to lack of exercise many brothers' and sisters' spirits have become extremely weak and flat, so that even when you encourage them to pray, their spirits cannot rise up. Therefore, we not only need to exercise our spirit at prayer time, but whenever something happens in our daily life we must return to our spirit, exercise our spirit concerning the matter, and then use the consciousness in our spirit to discern the situation. At such a time, the spirit must take the lead—the faculties of the soul must wait.

Some are so clear in thought and deep in thinking that whenever they meet a situation, the first organ they use is their mind, considering the matter over and over. This does not mean that it is wrong to use the mind. What it does mean is that to exercise the mind first and then the spirit, or even to exercise only the mind and not the spirit, is wrong in principle for a Christian. For a Christian, the principle in handling any matter is to first sense out the matter by exercising the spirit and then think it over with the mind. The mind should be a slave, an instrument, of the spirit. We should not allow the mind to take over; rather, we should allow our spirit to take the lead in touching every matter. For example, a brother may come to see you and talk with you. Your attitude should be to use your spirit first to contact and sense his situation; then use your mind to comprehend the consciousness in your spirit. Many people, whenever they meet someone or hear something, immediately exercise their mind to think and ponder. This is reversing the proper order. When we contact people or handle things it is especially important that we first exercise our spirit and then our mind.

The principle is the same concerning the will. Never use your will to make a decision concerning some matter and ignore the consciousness of your spirit. First sense it with your spirit, and then allow your will to serve as an instrument of the spirit to make the decision for you. In making any decision, we should submit our will wholly to the control of the spirit.

This is also true with the emotion. The sisters are usually full of emotion. Many times a sister's spirit is not strong because it has been subdued by her emotion. Emotion includes numerous elements, such as human preferences, hatred, fear, boldness, and so on. Never consider that all sisters are timid. Sometimes the sisters are bolder than the brothers, because they are more in their emotion. When the sisters are for something they are so bold that they fear neither heaven nor earth. But sometimes when they are afraid of something they are afraid to the extent that they do not care about reasons or anything else. All of this is something of the emotion. Therefore, if we want to learn how to be a proper Christian, in every situation we must first turn to our spirit and sense how it feels about that particular matter. We must keep this principle in our daily life, which includes our actions, our attitude toward others, our help to others, and even our service in the church. We should not say, "This is good, why don't we do it?" It is not a matter of good or bad, but it is a matter of what our spirit says. No matter how good something seems, if our spirit does not sanction such an action, we should not do it. By all means, we must allow our spirit to take the lead in all things.

Let us give a further explanation. When someone brings a matter to you, you should not let either your preference or fear take the lead. You must not approve the matter simply because you like it, refuse it because you are afraid of it, or put it aside because you are disgusted with it. Rather, you should first use your spirit to touch the matter, and allow your spirit to take the lead, overcoming the liking and approval, fear and distaste, and even the mind and will of your soul. Toward every thing that is set before you, always first exercise your spirit. In order to be a proper Christian, we need to have a strong spirit. In everything we need to exercise our spirit. I may not like a particular person, but if he comes to see me today, by all means, I must touch the consciousness in my spirit. I should not react according to my particular preference or distaste but according to my spirit.

I believe, brothers and sisters, you are clear about this point. May you henceforth put it into practice so that your spirit can become the strongest part in your whole being. I once saw a child learning to play the piano spend many hours each practice time. He practiced continually until his hands became the most skillful parts of his body, and his piano playing was excellent. The strongest part of a Christian should be his spirit. When our spirit is strong and living, we can pray well. However, just to know the teaching is useless; it is an absolute necessity that we faithfully put it into practice.

III. THE SPIRIT MUST BE PURE

Strictly speaking, the spirit itself is not easily defiled. Any uncleanness of the spirit is due to its being contaminated by the soul and body while passing through them to come forth. For example, if your mind is defiled, when your spirit passes through the mind to come forth, the defilement of your mind becomes the defilement of your spirit. If your emotion is unclean, when your spirit comes forth it will surely be contaminated with the uncleanness of the emotion. If your will is improper, when your spirit comes forth, it also becomes an improper spirit. For example, water may be very pure at its source, but if it passes through some material containing sulfur it will pick up some sulfuric element and eventually flow out as sulfuric water. Just so, it is not easy for the spirit to have contamination of itself. Rather, the defilement of the spirit is usually the result of the spirit's passing through our being.

Hence, in order for the spirit to be pure, man's mind, emotion, and will must be pure. One who has a peculiar mind will surely evidence a peculiar spirit. If one is very emotional and does not know how to control his passion—pleasure, anger, sorrow, or joy—when his spirit moves, it is unstable and uncontrollable. You may say that is something of the spirit. Yes, it may be so; for at that time elements of the emotions have been mixed with the spirit. But, strictly speaking, it is still not the spirit itself; rather, it is something of the emotion that has been mixed with the spirit. Someone may have a very obstinate and stubborn will. When his spirit comes forth, it will certainly be an obstinate and stubborn spirit. This is inevitable. Whatever kind of person you are, it is easy for your spirit to bear that flavor. If your faculties are not pure, your spirit will also be impure. In order that the spirit might be pure, the person himself must be pure. When the spirit of one who hates comes forth, his spirit expresses that hatred. So it is with one whose thought is unclean. When his spirit comes forth it will inevitably be unclean.

Once your spirit is impure you will have a bad conscience, and once you have a bad conscience your spirit will suffer total bankruptcy. It is not possible for such a spirit to pray. Thus, in order to have a spirit of prayer, the primary requirement is that you be a pure person. When one is pure, then his spirit is pure. Only one who has a pure spirit can have a good conscience. A good conscience will enable him to be strengthened in spirit and become a man of prayer.

IV. THE SPIRIT MUST BE FRESH, NOT OLD AND STALE

Many times in the prayer meeting or at the Lord's table, a brother or sister may have stood up to pray and made you feel that his spirit was very old. Every time such a one prays, although he may be chronologically young, you have a sense within that his spirit is old. And since it is old, it is stale. An old, stale spirit cannot pray.

A spirit of prayer is a fresh spirit. Such were the spirits of men of prayer in the Scripture. For example, Nehemiah, Ezra, Daniel, and Abraham were all men of prayer. And when you read their prayers, you can sense the freshness of their spirit. Some confessed their sins, while others repented deeply before God. Take, for example, Psalm 51, which is David's prayer of confession. In that psalm he was full of repentance and under a deep sense of condemnation, yet you still can sense that his spirit was fresh.

Please remember, a fresh spirit comes from a pure spirit. Every fresh spirit, therefore, is the result of many severe dealings before God. The more the dealings, the fresher the spirit. The reason a brother's or sister's spirit of prayer is stale is because he has not had any dealings with God for a long time. This is just like walking into a room that has not been cleaned for a month: immediately you feel everything is old and stale. But go and observe the Japanese homes. Many of the Japanese clean and wash their houses within and without almost every morning. When you go into such a house, or just walk past the door, you can feel the freshness.

Without dealings, there is staleness; with dealings, there is freshness. To this day you and I are still in the old creation. We still live among men of the old creation, and in an unclean, dark age on this corrupt, evil earth. We do not realize how much our spirit has been covered with the dust of this old creation and corrupt age. Even if we don't get ourselves defiled by it, this dust automatically falls into our being, causing our spirit to become old. Therefore, in order to maintain the purity of our person there must be the daily dealings. When there is the purity, then there is the freshness; when there is the freshness inside, the spirit can pray.

V. THE SPIRIT MUST BE BUOYANT

A fresh spirit is surely a buoyant spirit. If you do not have regular dealings before the Lord, your spirit cannot be fresh. A spirit that is not fresh is invariably depressed and is definitely unable to pray. Even if by the exercise of your will you force yourself to utter some words, or you use your mind to think of something to say, it is still futile. Therefore, whether you can pray and how much you can pray depend upon whether your spirit is depressed or buoyant. This is a real test.

VI. THE SPIRIT MUST BE LIVELY

That which is pure is fresh, that which is fresh is buoyant, and that which is buoyant surely is lively. Only such a spirit can pray. The moment you open your mouth others can sense whether or not the spirit in you is leaping and living. By contrast, you may have heard a brother pray and felt that his prayer was dead. Although he prayed, his spirit did not move. It was neither living nor released, but dead. It is not possible for such a spirit to pray. Thus, in order to be able to pray, the spirit must be lively, full of vitality.

VII. THE SPIRIT MUST BE FREE

Freedom means having no bondage or anxiety. Once you are anxious over a certain matter you cannot pray. You keep worrying about your son who is studying abroad, your wife who is being treated in the hospital, and your business that is not making money. Since your spirit is bound by these many things it cannot be free, and you are thus unable to pray. Even these good things can cause your spirit to be bound. On the other hand, there are still some whose spirits are captured by the theater, being bound by the movies. Thus, the spirit is bound and unable to pray. To the extent that our spirit is not freed from everything that is outside God there is no way for us to pray. Therefore, one who wishes to learn how to pray must exercise his spirit, making it able to be independent at all times—bound neither by the attraction of that which is good nor by that which is bad. Regardless how difficult, how heavy, or how troublesome the matter may be, your spirit can remain free and unbothered. A spirit that can pray is one that is not bound and entangled but is transcendent and free.

VIII. THE SPIRIT MUST BE LIGHT AND EASY

The spirit must not only be free; it must also be easy. When praying, you must learn not to bear burdens that are too heavy. One who is heavy-laden can never pray. True, the spirit should not be lazy, but neither should it be over-loaded. Freedom means to have no bondage; whereas, easiness means to have no heavy burden. Freedom means to get out of all entanglements that are outside God; whereas easiness means to not bear too heavy a burden in the spirit. For example, you may go before God today to pray for two matters and be able to pray very well. However, if you bear five things with you while you pray, you cannot pray well, because the things, being too many and too heavy, have caused your spirit to become completely worn out. It is just like an ordinary person who may be able to walk well when he is carrying a fifty-pound load, but who is not able to walk if he is bearing a five-hundred-pound load.

Therefore, in prayer, we need to guard against laziness in our spirit. However, at the same time we need to prevent our spirit from being over diligent and taking too heavy a load, thus falling into uneasiness. We need to maintain a balanced spirit which is neither lazy nor overdiligent. Take only the burden that you can bear, so that your spirit will be light. This should be our attitude in prayer.

Of course, there are times when burdens would press us into fasting and prayer, but that is another matter. In ordinary times, we need to allow our spirit to feel at ease and not be pressed continually. A spirit that is not free cannot pray; neither can a spirit that is not light pray well. One who prays well always exercises his spirit, keeping it free and light.

IX. THE SPIRIT MUST BE RESTFUL AND CALM

One cannot pray if his spirit has no rest and is always in turmoil. When hearing joyful or sorrowful news, some get very excited in their spirit and cannot calm down. This stimulation, which results from either joy or sorrow, can make one unable to pray. Therefore, we must train ourselves so that whether a situation we encounter is happy or sad, our spirit will not be too excited or stirred up. A spirit cannot pray if it is restless or in turmoil.

Seriously speaking, if we are well-trained to pray then we have learned a great deal before the Lord. If the organs of our body need exercise in order to be useful, then, much more, our spirit needs to be exercised in order to function. Prayer requires learning the lessons—especially the lesson of the proper exercise of the spirit. If you can always maintain a calm and peaceful spirit in any situation or circumstance and with anyone, then you can pray.

X. THE SPIRIT MUST BE OPEN

A spirit of prayer is also an open spirit. Once the spirit is closed it cannot pray. The spirit should be open toward God, toward the brothers and sisters, and also toward others. But this does not mean that our spirit is never closed. Sometimes it needs to be closed. Our spirit should be able to close as well as open. This is just like a proper and frequently-used door which opens and closes flexibly according to the need. However, some doors are not frequently used and, therefore, are difficult to open and close. It is hard to open them, and once they are opened, they cannot be closed. With respect to their spirit, some brothers and sisters are just like this. Such a person cannot pray. In order to pray, the spirit must have the ability to open and close with flexibility. It should be able at any time to open toward God and men. When it should be closed, it should do so automatically. A spirit that opens and closes properly is an open spirit. Within a brief space of time it may open and close several times.

When one whose spirit opens freely contacts others and talks to them, after only one or two sentences, his spirit opens. This in turn causes the spirit of the others to also open. Only someone with such a spirit is able to lead people to salvation and to render help to others. Sometimes a brother may speak to someone for ten minutes. If the brother's spirit is not open, whatever he would speak or pray is vain. Thus, in order to have a proper prayer, the spirit must be open.

XI. THE SPIRIT MUST BE TRANSCENDENT

To be transcendent means to be risen above the different parts of the soul—mind, emotion, and will—and not to be under their control. A spirit that is transcendent is able to pray normally, and at the same time, it is able to be released to the degree that it ought. If you allow the various parts of your soul to dominate your spirit even a little, you are defeated in prayer. Thus, in prayer always allow the spirit to transcend everything. You need to allow your spirit to be both the strongest and the highest part of your being. You are then a man of prayer.

XII. THE SPIRIT MUST BE STABLE

Our spirit should not be buoyant and transcendent one day and depressed the next day. Neither should it be so free this minute and so bound the next minute. Stability of the spirit means that the spirit is not affected by any circumstance but is always steadfast before the Lord.

The weather in Taiwan fluctuates a great deal. It may be calm and windless in the morning, and yet a typhoon may come in the evening. You may need a sweater in the morning but only a shirt at noon. This is instability. Such are the spirits of some of the brothers and sisters. Yesterday your fellowship with a certain brother was wonderful and the prayer was excellent. However, today when you see him his whole being is collapsed, and he has become helpless. Such an unstable person cannot pray. In order to pray the spirit must remain balanced and stable: free, yet stable; transcendent, yet stable; buoyant, yet stable. We need to be exercised that our spirits may manifest these characteristics.

CHAPTER SIX

THE MIND OF PRAYER

I. THE POSITION OF THE MIND

We all know that man was created with three parts: spirit, soul, and body. The soul is the medium between the spirit and the body. The soul is our personality, our ego. Within the soul, the leading part is the mind. Both the emotion and the will are subordinate to the mind. Man's going forth and coming in hinge on the mind. Going forth is his expression, and coming in is his reception. Whether we express what is within us or receive what is without, both need to pass through the mind. Thus, the mind not only occupies the leading position in the soul, but is also a very significant part of our whole being.

Christians use the word "mind" as a specific term in relation to biblical truth. When talking about the mind, unbelievers refer to it as the brain or the psyche. The term "brain" is used in reference to the physical entity, and the term "psyche" is used in reference to the psychological entity. Worldly education educates the human brain, or psyche. Every kind of knowledge, whether science, philosophy, ism, or any theory, deals with the human brain, and/or psyche. According to the present educational system, one needs at least twenty years of formal education before he can obtain a bachelor's degree. It requires twenty years of training to sufficiently develop the human brain to make it useful for human living. By this we can see how important a position it occupies in man.

If the mind needs to be educated for our human living, how much more it needs to be trained for prayer. Unless it has been educated, the mind can neither receive nor discharge the burden of prayer. Whether a person desires to receive or discharge a burden in prayer, a functional mind is necessary. Although prayer issues forth from the spirit, it must pass through the mind. Once the mind becomes improper, there is a problem with prayer. Thus, in order to be a man of prayer, it is imperative that we pay attention to the exercise of our mind.

II. THE RENEWING OF THE MIND

The Scriptures show us that due to the fall of man the human mind has become darkened and numb. Because man sinned, his mind became vain and perverted. Therefore, he does not take heed of the things that he ought but rather of the things that he ought not. Today, concerning the matter of committing sins, man has a very clever mind, but concerning the matter of seeking God and listening to His truths, his mind is very inadequate. This proves that the mind of a sinning one is darkened and perverted. Thus, Romans 12:2 says, "be transformed by the renewing of the mind."

At the time of our regeneration our spirit became renewed by the entrance of the Spirit of God into it. Thereafter the Holy Spirit began to spread out from our spirit into the various parts of our soul, especially into our mind. The Holy Spirit shines forth the light from our spirit to enlighten our mind, dispel its darkness, and correct its perverseness. This dispelling of the darkness and correcting of the perverseness are the renewing work of the Holy Spirit in our mind.

In renewing our mind, God not only corrects it and shines into it through the Holy Spirit in our spirit; He also gives us His Holy Word, the Bible, outwardly. When we read the Bible, it is not just to touch God and know His heart. It is also that through the Word our darkened mind may be enlightened, our perverted thoughts may be corrected, and our old mentality may be renewed. Alas, sometimes in reading the Word, instead of reading the Word into himself, one reads himself into the Word. Such a one does not have a humble heart to receive instruction and correction from the Word. On the contrary, his intention is to read his own views and ideas into the Word. Thus, he does not allow the Word to renew his mind and loses the real benefit of reading it.

Anyone who desires to read the Word properly should learn to lay aside his views and abandon his ideas. He should come to the Word in a humble manner and without prejudice. If we come to the Word with such an attitude, we can receive the teachings of the Word into us. Once the biblical teachings get into us, the ideas, views, and opinions in our mind will be changed. The Holy Scripture from without corresponds to the Holy Spirit within to enlighten our mind and correct our mentality. This causes our darkened, perverted mind to be renewed.

Therefore, with one who loves the Lord and walks according to the Spirit, the more he reads the Word and is instructed by the Word, the more intelligent and proper his mind becomes. He will become dull in evil things, but very alive in spiritual matters. Only a mind that has been thus renewed can cooperate with the spirit of prayer to pray.

III. THE SOBRIETY OF THE MIND

A mind that has been renewed should be very clean and bright. Such a mind is also surely transparent. Sometimes it is impossible to talk with certain brothers or sisters concerning spiritual things because their mind is neither clear nor bright. Rather, it is all mixed up just like paste. A person with such a mentality is unable to discern between the head or tail of anything. To him, there is not much difference between eight and nine, nor is there much difference between nine and ten. How can someone like this pray? If his mind is confused, surely he will not be able to pray with clarity.

Please read the examples of prayer in the Bible. You will find that none of those who prayed spoke silly words. Hannah, the mother of Samuel, is a good example. Following the birth of Samuel, she went before God to offer her thanksgiving. It is unlikely that Hannah had much education, because there was no girls' school among the Israelites at that time. However, when you read her utterance in prayer, you can sense that she not only had a shining spirit, but also a sober mind. Since her mind was as clear as a glass window, the Spirit of God could directly utter words of prayer through her spirit in a clear way.

In the New Testament there was another mother, Mary, the mother of the Lord Jesus. Being of a humble background, she was not highly educated. Her prayer, however, demonstrates that her mind was also very sober and her thinking was not at all confused. Confused prayers are the products of confused minds. Because of God's mercy, He may answer many nonsensical prayers. Nevertheless, one should not be content with praying silly prayers, thinking that one way or the other God will always listen. This attitude is wrong. All those who know prayer realize that many times when we go before God to pray, it is like handling diplomatic affairs or defending a case in court. A lawyer knows that when defending his client his mind must be clear and his words must be sober. A sober speech is based on his ability to understand as well as to speak forth clearly. Thus, in order to be a man of prayer, we need a mind that is renewed and sober. The renewing of the mind is the work of the Holy Spirit through the Word. But in order to have a sober mind we ourselves need to be responsible to exercise it.

IV. THE CONCENTRATION OF THE MIND

Our mind should not only be sober, but should also be able to concentrate well. I believe many brothers and sisters have realized that the biggest problem in our prayer is a desultory mind, a mind which does not easily concentrate but always drifts about. When some brothers and sisters kneel down to pray, in less than five minutes their minds begin to travel around the world. One moment they think of the United States, then their thoughts move on to Great Britain, and later they think of Hong Kong. Their minds cannot be focused, and their thoughts fly everywhere and go every place.

I believe we have all had this experience. The reason we are unable to pray is that our thoughts continually drift. We cannot either collect or direct them. It is very strange that this does not happen while we read the Bible or talk with people. However, for some unexplainable reason, whenever we pray it seems that a telegraph inside keeps transmitting messages until we become disabled in prayer. This is what is referred to as being scatterbrained. We may not be aware of having a mind that is not sober, but we are very clear concerning what it means to be scatterbrained. Once our thoughts become scattered, we cannot pray. Thus, in order to pray, we must have a proper concentration.

To gain a proper concentration requires regular exercise. The way to properly exercise your mind is to control your thinking, not allowing your thoughts to run wild. Some people are too loose and free in their thinking. Such a person indulges his mind, exercising no control or restriction over it whatsoever. The mind of such a one is like a wild horse running loose without a bridle. Not only is that person unable to pray, but he is also unable to read the Bible. Learn to control your mind, and do not allow it to fall into fanciful thinking. Always restrict your mind to not think beyond its proper limit, but think only of the things that pertain to your duty or responsibility. For example, if you are going to visit a friend today, you need to exercise your mind a little to consider which way to go, the means of transportation, the best time to go, what to do there, and when to come back. Because this kind of thinking pertains to your responsibility, it is proper. But sometimes you allow yourself to think of things about which you should not be thinking. At such a time, you need to restrict yourself. At times you may find yourself unable to restrict your thoughts. Then I would suggest that you perform some chores or read a book. Whenever you discover that your mind is running wild, try your best to keep yourself busy. The more you let it go, the more wild your mind becomes. Such indulgence makes you unable to pray.

Also, many times thoughts which are not our own may come into our mind. These are darts shot from outside. These darting thoughts also distract our mind and disturb our prayer. Hence, we must learn to refuse them. Even though they may return after you refuse them, do not receive them. Sometimes, the more you refuse those darting thoughts, the fiercer they become. This is like mischievous children knocking at your door. The more you tell them not to knock, the louder they knock. At that time, you can stop refusing them and just ignore them. In the same way, by refusing and ignoring those thoughts, they too will just go away.

In summary, to properly concentrate we need to practice the control of our thinking and refuse the darting thoughts. After such practice, our mind will spontaneously be directed in a proper way; then when we again kneel down to pray our mind will respond to our direction and will be able to concentrate.

V. THE STILLNESS OF THE MIND

One who knows how to pray can usually quietly rest his mind. Not only is he able to concentrate with his mind, but he can also quiet his thinking. It is just like the rest sign in music. A pianist coming to a rest sign first pauses and then goes on. It is also similar to the term "selah" in the Psalms, which designates a certain time of silence. Sometimes our prayer before God needs to come to a halt. We need to train and control our mind to such an extent that we can think, pause, concentrate, and obey at will. Thus, we can be a man of prayer.

The stillness of the mind is not only a pause in the mind's activities, but also includes resting one's mind. One whose thinking never ceases uses his mind to excess and will experience a very difficult time in prayer because his mind cannot be still. Many times we are unable to pray before going to bed at night. This is also due to the fact that our mind has hardly stopped during the day and is exhausted. The spirit desires to pray, but the mind is tired and cannot be used. This is very damaging to prayer. Thus, in order to pray, it is necessary that you frequently still your mind. You not only need to refrain from foolish thinking and vain imaginings, but sometimes you need to stop even the proper use of the mind. Always reserve a portion of your mental capacity for the purpose of prayer. If the mind is not properly controlled there will be a problem in prayer.

VI. SETTING THE MIND ON SPIRITUAL THINGS

With regard to the control of the mind, both concentration and rest are negative aspects. The positive aspect of exercising the mind is to set the mind on spiritual things. It is not easy to stop our mind. Psychologists tell us that even in our sleep our mind does not rest. Therefore, we need to place more stress on the positive aspect of exercising our mind. In addition to performing the normal duties, during leisure times one should use his mind to think concerning the spiritual things. This is minding the things of the Spirit (Rom. 8:5). When the mind is unoccupied, you need to set it upon spiritual things.

Of course, even while setting the mind on spiritual things, we must refrain from fanciful thinking. Formerly there was a sister in northern China who always imagined herself to be Madame Guyon. She always sat there, closed her eyes, and engaged in vain imaginations. Yet she thought she was fellowshipping with the Lord. She said, "I wish to renew the marriage vow between the Lord and me." She also said, "I would choose the cross, not any easiness." In such a way she engaged herself in fanciful thinking. This departs from the normal way of minding spiritual things. In order to set the mind on spiritual things in a normal way, you need to think in the proper way. For example, you may think of the Word, consider the beauty of the Lord or His works, or reflect on how the Spirit leads within us. We need to think on these spiritual things.

Some brothers inquired of me why they are short of utterance in ministering the Word. I always like to answer in this way: "It is because, ordinarily, you never consider the spiritual things. Either you think about the flood in the middle part of Taiwan, or you remember that spinach used to sell at a yen per pound but has now gone up to three yens. You are continually thinking about these earthly things. Because you have been thinking about these things, when you give a message you are short of utterance. If you still would not adequately restrict your thinking, I am afraid that one day the words 'spinach is selling at three yen per pound' will slip out of your mouth while you are ministering the Word. Because you think only of these things and do not mind the spiritual things, your mind becomes very dull. So it is with prayer. When some people speak a humorous word or a satirical and mocking word their two lips are very sharp, but if you want them to pray their mind becomes inoperative."

I wish to tell you, brothers and sisters, that utterance in ministering the Word is a deposit being built up daily by minding the spiritual things. Whenever you have some leisure time, consider the things of the Spirit such as: what is the dealing of the flesh? what is the dealing of the self? what is the difference between the dealing of the self and the dealing of the flesh? and why in the Bible does it sometimes say that our old man has been crucified and other times say that our flesh has been crucified? If you think on these things, you will become well-versed and skillful within. When the time for ministering the Word comes, spontaneously you will have the inner, instant utterance because for a long time you have been building up spiritual riches which you can use at any time. Hence, train your mind so that it is always set on the spiritual things.

VII. THE RULING OF THE SPIRIT OVER THE MIND

Within our whole being, the supreme part is the spirit; the spirit is the master of our whole being. Although the spirit should subject itself to the Lord's ruling, it still stands in the chief position in the whole being. The spirit dominates the soul, and through the soul it dominates the body; thus, the mind must yield itself to the control of the spirit. One must always exercise so that the spirit may direct his mind. Of course, we admit that this is not an easy thing to do. It is not easy to focus our mind, and it is even harder for our spirit to rule our mind, for some have never learned how to exercise their spirit nor how to use their spiritual sense, the consciousness of the spirit. Not only are the unbelievers like this, but Christians are, also. All those who do not know how to exercise their spirit have a dominating mind. If your mind dominates your spirit you cannot pray. Only when you always allow the spirit to have the preeminence, ruling and controlling the mind, can the mind really be useful in spiritual things. Often we exhort people to pray, yet it is of no avail. There are numerous reasons that a person is unable to pray, but the chief reason is that the mind is not standing in the proper position. The mind has surpassed the spirit, and having upset the order, has risen from the position of a slave to become the master.

Let us give an illustration of how to practice allowing the spirit to rule the mind. Suppose someone comes to see you. While listening to his talking, use your spirit to sense before exercising your mind to think. Wait until there is the consciousness in your spirit; then allow the spirit to direct the mind to comprehend and express that consciousness. This is what is meant by letting the spirit be lord, ruling the mind. But commonly, when we talk with others, we put our spirit aside, letting it remain inoperative, and we allow our mind to go into full function. If in our daily life the mind climbs too high while the spirit descends too low, when prayer time comes it will not be easy for the spirit to rise again. Hence, in our daily living, we need to practice continually not allowing the mind to dominate the spirit, but rather allowing the spirit to rule and direct the mind. Thus, we will be able to pray well.

VIII. THE MIND OF THE SPIRIT

Romans 8:6 tells us that our mind may be of the flesh or of the spirit. The mind of the flesh refers to the mind standing on the side of the flesh and being ruled by the flesh. The mind of the spirit refers to the mind standing on the side of the spirit, cooperating with the spirit, being ruled by the spirit, and minding the spiritual things. Romans 8:5-6 says, "For those who are according to flesh mind the things of the flesh; but those who are according to spirit, the things of the Spirit. For the mind set on the flesh is death, but the mind set on the spirit is life and peace." In verse 5 the word mind is used as a verb. In verse 6, concerning the same thing, it is used as a noun, that is, the mind of the spirit. When your mind is ruled by the spirit, submits to the spirit, and always minds the things of the spirit, the mind is spiritual and becomes the mind of the spirit. Only the mind set on the spirit can cause you to touch life and have peace within. A mind of prayer is one that minds the spirit, cooperates with the spirit, submits itself to the ruling of the spirit, and is set on the spirit. Only such a mind can pray competently and properly.

IX. THE SPIRIT OF THE MIND

Ephesians 4:23 says, "And are renewed in the spirit of your mind." The spirit of the mind denotes the presence of the spirit in the mind. The spirit has entered into the mind. Formerly the spirit was the spirit and the mind was the mind, but now the spirit and the mind have joined and are mingled as one. Not only has the spirit been renewed, and not only has the mind been renewed, but the spirit and the mind have been mingled together and are completely renewed. This is the meaning of Ephesians 4:23. In other words, there is a mind that can never be separated from the spirit. It is not only a mind of the spirit, submitting itself to the rule of the spirit, being directed by the spirit, and minding the things of the spirit, but it has the element of the spirit within and is mingled with the spirit. When it thinks, the spirit is in its thinking. The elements of the spirit are found in its every movement. When a person reaches this stage he is rather deep in the Lord. His spirit has spread to his soul, his soul is under the control of the spirit, and the mind of the soul has the elements of the spirit within. Such a one is surely able to pray.

I believe that the brothers and sisters will have a better understanding if I add a few more words. In reading the prayers in the Bible, you can sense that the spirit is there. At the same time, you can also sense that the thinking of the mind is there. You can sense the presence of the spirit in such a mind. For example, if you read Daniel's prayer of confession in chapter nine, you can see that the words are full of clear thoughts proceeding from a sober mind. At the same time, they are full of the spirit, because the spirit and the mind are mingled together and the mind is filled with the elements of the spirit. This is the mind of the spirit. We need such a mind in order to pray. Many times when the brothers and sisters are praying they have only the thoughts but not the spirit. At other times, when they have a considerable amount of the elements of the spirit, their thinking is poor, incoherent, and inadequate. This proves that they have not been renewed in the spirit of their mind.

X. THE MIND INTERPRETING THE CONSCIOUSNESS OF THE SPIRIT

Once there is consciousness in the spirit, it is necessary for the mind to interpret it. The consciousness in the spirit is usually very fine. Therefore, in order that the mind might be able to interpret it, it is necessary that one pay attention to the foregoing eight items: (1) to be renewed, (2) sober, (3) concentrating, (4) still, (5) minding the things of the spirit, (6) ruled by the spirit, (7) having a mind of the spirit, and (8) filling the mind with the elements of the spirit. At this point the mind can understand the spiritual burden and interpret the spiritual sense.

For example, in a prayer meeting, you have a burden to pray, yet you are not clear how to pray. This means you do not know the meaning of that particular burden, and there are not enough elements of the spirit in your mind. But if at this particular time your mind is spiritual, having been trained, immediately you can comprehend and express the burden adequately. The same principle applies to the ministry of the Word. I may have a burden to speak a word to the brothers and sisters, but it requires the cooperation of and the interpretation by the mind in order to find out the meaning of the particular burden and sense in the spirit.

All good prayers come about by first having the consciousness and burden in the spirit. We must have a very sharp mind which is capable of fully expressing that spiritual consciousness with very fine words and rich thoughts. Some brothers and sisters are full of feeling within and rich in spiritual sense, yet their mind cannot interpret. All they can do is shout a great deal and weep or laugh. They have the feeling and the burden, but their mind is inadequate.

Around 1947, the meetings in Shanghai had begun to undergo a revival. During a breaking-bread meeting on one Lord's day afternoon, a brother who was a native of southern Fookien was inspired and prayed with his native tongue to express the inspiration within. While listening, although I was not able to understand too well, I could tell that even in his native dialect he could not adequately express the inspiration within. So, he simply turned red, his body shook, and his eyes shed tears. The whole congregation was aware that he had the feelings, but unfortunately, due to the lack of the cooperation of the mind, he did not have the appropriate words to express them. If his mind had been trained, and he could have spoken either Mandarin or Shanghainese, using rich words to pour out all the feeling within, I believe that the whole meeting would have exploded. However, it was regrettable that because his untrained mind could not interpret what was within him, it could not explode to the outside. Therefore, brothers, if we wish to pray properly, we need to exercise so that our mind will be able to match and interpret the feelings in our spirit. This is essential.

XI. THE SPIRITUAL EXPRESSION OF THE MIND

The mind must not only be able to interpret the consciousness in the spirit, but it also needs to have the words to express that consciousness. This is the matter of utterance. Those who have acted as interpreters know that this is not easy. To be able to comprehend and express the consciousness in the spirit immediately is not easy. Sometimes we have understood what is in our spirit, but we were unable to express it. At another time, we have expressed it yet others could not understand it. The proper understanding and expression require exercise. Paul asked the saints to pray on his behalf that utterance would be given unto him (Eph. 6:19). The utterance Paul was referring to was not a fluency or eloquence of speech in ordinary conversation, but the ability to express the feelings that were within him. Such utterance is related to the mind.

There are some brothers whose minds have been trained in this way. When they pray with several others they are not only able to express the feelings within themselves, but also the feelings within everyone else. Hence, when they pray, once the words come forth everyone feels released, for the prayer of such a one has released everyone's spirits. But if someone who has not been trained in his mind prays, the more he prays, the more others are uncomfortable and even smothered within. They feel most miserable. The more he prays the more the spirits of others are frustrated; for his mind, not having been trained, is unable to find a suitable expression. Therefore, if you wish to pray well it is absolutely necessary that you train your mind. Train yourself so that your mind can comprehend the consciousness in the spirit and find the right utterance to express it instantly.

XII. THE PRAYER OF THE MIND

When you have all the above points you can pray with your mind. First Corinthians 14:15 calls this "praying with the understanding." The word "understanding" there has the same root as the word "mind." The understanding is the mind. To pray with the spirit refers to speaking in tongues, which does not need to pass through the mind. But the apostle Paul said that, in the church, that kind of prayer is not as valuable as praying with the understanding, for the former cannot be understood by others, but the latter can. Therefore, in order to have prayers that can utter and express the feelings within—the prayers of the mind—your mind must be trained in the above points. The prayer of the mind is not only expressed from the mind, but even more it comes forth from the spirit, passing through the interpretation of the mind, and then is uttered as prayer.

CHAPTER SEVEN

THE EMOTION OF PRAYER

One who prays not only needs to have a proper spirit, but the various parts of his soul also need to be normal. If we wish to learn to pray properly, we need to adjust our entire being. We should realize that we are fallen human beings, and that not one part of our being is altogether sound. Never think that all the problems of our being have been resolved by regeneration. It is not that simple. Although regeneration has made our spirit alive, the various other parts of our being are still not exactly right, or proper. Therefore, they need to be readjusted. It is because our mind is still not proper that the Scriptures tell us a saved person still needs to be renewed in his mind. This renewing includes almost all matters related to the adjustment of the mind. However, the Bible also tells us to, "Rejoice with those who rejoice, and weep with those who weep" (Rom. 12:15). This is a matter concerning the adjustment of the emotion. Some do not have a proper emotion. They do not rejoice when they should be rejoicing, nor weep when they should be weeping. Such emotion is unsuitable if one is to be a normal Christian. If it is necessary to have an adjusted emotion for our human walk, then how much more needful it is to have an adjusted emotion for prayer.

Prayer is man coming with his whole being before God to engage in a serious matter. If there is any part in you that is improper, then you cannot be a normal, proper, and correct praying one. For example, suppose your emotion is shown to be improper because you only like exciting and noisy prayer. All the examples of prayer in the Bible show us that every man of prayer had an upright spirit, sober mind, and proper emotions. Their emotions, undoubtedly, had been trained and adjusted.

Generally speaking, modern educators pay most of their attention to educating the human mind. They seldom give heed to cultivating the human emotions. Even if they do cultivate the emotions, it is often by means of varieties of perverted and rough music. Under such influence the human emotions become even more improper. Therefore, we can say that human education with all its methods has not paid attention to the matter of properly adjusting the emotion. Human emotion is also a part within man that is very much fallen and has been very much damaged. We have to admit that many mistakes, sins, and corruptions are not necessarily works of the human mind. Instead, they are produced by the emotion, which tricks us into doing many improper things. Therefore, if we wish to be a proper Christian, as well as a man of prayer before God, not only do we need to heed the matter of the mind as mentioned in the previous chapter, but we also need to consider this matter of a correct emotion.

I. THE POSITION OF THE EMOTION

The emotion is a part of the soul and ranks below the mind and the will. In other words, the emotion should be under the control of the will and the mind. We often say that we should not do things according to our emotions. This means we should not yield to our emotion, but that the emotion should submit itself to the ruling of the sober mind and the proper will. If the emotion were to occupy the chief position and rule over everything, it is difficult to know how far we would be led astray. When we are happy, we can soar to the third heavens. When we are miserable, we do not even want to live any longer. But with a normal human, though he is rich in emotions, they are very much controlled by his mind. Both in the Bible and in daily life we can see that a proper human being is one whose emotion is definitely under the control of the will and the mind; and the more it is under the control of these faculties, the more such a person is normal and proper. If one's emotion is not under the rule of the mind and the will, it is just like a car that has no brakes.

As soon as it is driven, it gets into an accident. Furthermore, since it is under no regulation, it is difficult to tell how disastrously far it may go. This is a very dangerous matter. Hence, the position of the emotion is to be under the control of the mind and the will.

II. A MODERATE EMOTION

We often say that someone has an abundance of emotions, but someone else does not have much emotion and therefore is cold, like a man of wood or stone. Brothers and sisters, we need to see that to be over-abundant in emotions is wrong, and to be too cold in emotions is also wrong. Both are immoderate. A proper person is one who is moderate in pleasure, anger, sorrow, and joy. Whether he is happy or sad, there is a fixed degree. He laughs, but only to a certain extent. He weeps and is sorrowful only to a certain extent. His emotion is moderate and balanced.

Thirty years ago in a certain meeting in northern China I saw some conditions of immoderate emotions. When the brothers and sisters prayed the degree of excitement of some was beyond description. They shouted, clapped their hands, laughed, and trembled. They actually laughed to the point of going crazy. It is hard to find a word in the dictionary to describe that situation. I also saw one weeping in a way that was simply unimaginable. Even someone whose father or mother had died would not have cried with that kind of a voice. He wept with such great sorrow that it caused others to have a chilling sensation. These were displays of improper, excessive emotions. In 2 Corinthians 5, Paul tells us that we ought to be beside ourselves before God and be of a sober mind before man (v. 13). This is to regulate and temper our emotion.

Without a moderate emotion you cannot pray properly. It is not right to have immoderate emotion, nor is it right to be lacking in emotion. Some brothers and sisters who pray in the meetings are just like robots. They pray without any expression whatsoever and sound exactly like a typewriter. While the conditions which we described earlier show an excessive emotion, a condition such as this reveals a shortage of emotions. Both of these are conditions of an immoderate emotion.

Never consider this a small matter. In Bethany, when the Lord Jesus saw the condition of Mary and of the Jews and thought of the death of Lazarus, He wept. This, the shortest verse in the Bible, shows us that the Lord had emotions. However, in His weeping the Lord did not wail so as to cause those around Him to have a chilling sensation in their bones. The Scripture simply says this word: "Jesus wept" (John 11:35). By reading the record you can tell that He was One with a very moderate emotion. On another occasion, when He cleansed the temple, He made a scourge of cords and cast out all the sheep and the oxen, and overthrew the tables of the money-changers. We can say that He was thunderingly angry that day. But you cannot find any trace in the Bible indicating that on that day the Lord Jesus had made a great mess in the temple by breaking everything in it. With some brothers, if they do not lose their temper, all is well; but once they become angry, they create a big mess by breaking everything—the windows, teapot, etc. Oh, how moderate was the emotion of our Lord Jesus! If you and I wish to be normal Christians, our emotions need to be moderate. Whether we are happy or sad, it must only be to a certain degree.

III. A SOUND EMOTION

Man's emotion should not only be moderate, but also sound. Moderation is a matter concerning degree, while soundness is a matter concerning nature. You all know what we mean by soundness. With some brothers and sisters, when they laugh, it is a wicked laugh, and when they are sorrowful, it is a crooked sorrow. Their feelings of pleasure, anger, sorrow, and joy are not sound. Likewise, if a man can only laugh, but cannot weep, and never gets angry, he is most likely a false Christian. The Bible says, "Be angry, and do not sin" (Eph. 4:26). If one sins in his anger, his anger is unsound and evil. Some weep and laugh with propriety, but others cry and laugh in an unsound, unseemly manner. All these unsound emotions are obstacles to our prayers. Hence, if we wish to be a normal praying one, we need an emotion which is both moderate and sound.

IV. A REFINED EMOTION

To be refined means to be gentle, fine, and polite. A Christian's emotion should be cultured, not wild. He is polite, whether happy or sad. You can sense that he is very polite and lovable even in grief or in anger. These are areas where the emotion needs to be adjusted. Some brothers and sisters are really gracious and polite when they are on good terms with you, but once they are angry with you they look like demons coming out of the bottomless pit. This proves that their emotion is really not refined. And some even look ugly when they are excited, because they behave in a wild, loose manner. This means their emotion has not been adjusted. By the Lord's life, you and I need to exercise ourselves so that even in our anger there is refinement. I repeat, the emotion needs to be refined in order to have proper prayer.

V. A TEMPERATE, RESTRAINED EMOTION

To be temperate means to be mild and respectful. To be restrained means to be able to restrict oneself. Hence, to be temperate and restrained means that your emotion must always be respectful, polite, and under self-control. Do not cry with no restraint and lose your normality. Although you cry, you must still be respectful and polite, controlling and restraining yourself. Also, do not allow yourself to be unrestrained when you are angry. When you exercise your emotions, be temperate, respectful and polite, restrained and restricted. This is not merely a matter of being moderate, sound, and refined. Refinement simply means that the emotion of such a one is very polite and nice. Temperance and self-restraint mean that, in addition to politeness, there is also a kind of self-control, self-restriction.

Why do we need to use words like these? It is because the emotion is a very delicate matter. It is necessary to cover the very fine points in order to adjust our emotion. A normal Christian is not like a wooden man. Rather, he is full of emotions, always has a joyful countenance toward others, and is moderate, sound, refined, respectful and polite, self-restrained and self-controlled.

Sometimes you may come across a brother or sister who demonstrates no emotions. He never laughs or cries. This kind of person is like a piece of ice or stone. He is neither temperate nor restrained. On other occasions you may meet a brother or sister whose emotions are disorderly and unruly, like the uncombed hair in the morning. Both his laughing and crying are a mess—neither temperate, restrained, nor cultured. Such emotions are great frustrations to our prayers. If we wish to learn to pray, we need to learn these lessons concerning the emotion.

VI. A TRANQUIL EMOTION

Tranquility of emotion means that the emotion is able to remain calm. To be tranquil means to be serene; the two are almost synonymous. It is very easy for one who is emotional to be boiling in his emotions; hence, he must learn to calm his emotions. To be tranquil in this sense does not mean to be quiet; rather, it means to be calm or settled. For example, with some, once they hear some joyful news they become too excited and can no longer pray. Not only can they no longer pray, but they cannot even sit still inside the house. This means they do not have a calm emotion. Some are not able to pray after losing their temper or getting angry; this also indicates a disturbed emotion.

We often think that we are unable to pray because our mind has been disturbed. Actually, it is easy to overcome the disturbance of the mind. If we can maintain a tranquil emotion, we will not be affected even though someone beside us may say something. But once our emotion is stirred up, it will be very difficult for us to get into our spirit to pray. Sometimes this may continue for days before we can pray again.

A disturbed emotion will adversely affect our prayer life. When some are happy, they will cry and laugh in their prayer and even forget about eating. But when they become unhappy, they can stop praying for one week. Their prayer life is unpredictable, being entirely under the control of their emotion. Such a one whose emotion is not tranquil cannot pray. Hence, we need to exercise to be tranquil.

VII. A CONTROLLED EMOTION

All the aforementioned lessons are for the purpose of controlling the emotion. To control the emotion does not mean it becomes a pretense. It is still very real. The laugh of a diplomat is an entirely false laugh, and his sympathy for others is also not real. What we mean by a controlled emotion is not the false emotion of a diplomat. Rather, it is genuine but regulated, not raw, wild, loose, or without limitation. An emotion that is thus being controlled is restricted, regulated, and disciplined. Unless the emotion has learned these lessons, it is very difficult for our prayer life to last very long.

VIII. A SPIRITUAL EMOTION

If your emotion has been adjusted so that it is moderate, sound, refined, temperate, restrained, tranquil, and controlled, then you will be able to bring the entire emotion into subjection to the spirit. It will then be ruled by the spirit. Your emotion will not move independently, but will have its head entirely covered before the spirit, allowing the spirit to be the head. When the spirit rejoices, it rejoices. When the spirit is grieved, it is grieved. Whenever the spirit makes a move, the emotion also makes a move. It always follows the spirit. Only an emotion that is sound, moderate, refined, temperate and restrained, tranquil, and able to exercise self-control can be directed by the spirit. At this point, the emotion becomes a spiritual emotion.

I believe, brothers and sisters, if you are without prejudice and are willing to calmly think over these points, you will find out that the cause of numerous problems in your spiritual life lies with the emotion. Why is it you cannot pray for long? Why is your spiritual life before God not so normal, but suddenly high and then suddenly low? It is because your emotion has not been adjusted so as to become moderate, sound, refined, temperate and restrained, tranquil, and always under control. You have not been able to make your emotion subject to the leading of the spirit. Your emotion is individualistic and is dominating the spirit. Your being is continuously being disturbed by the emotion. Hence, in order to be a proper man of prayer, the emotion must subject itself to the spirit, allowing the spirit to occupy the first place. Thus, you will be able to maintain a normal prayer life.

IX. THE EMOTION AND THE SPIRIT

Here we will consider the function of the emotion and its relation to the spirit. We know that the emotion is the organ by which man expresses himself. The mind affords man a way of expression by causing him to know how to express himself, but it is man's emotion that directly expresses the man himself. Likewise, God expresses Himself to a considerable extent from our spirit through our mind, but to an even greater extent He expresses Himself through our emotion. When one prays, it is the faculty of the emotion that directly utters the burden in the spirit. For example, the Holy Spirit may give you a feeling of sorrow and repentance, yet you are void of a sorrowful emotion and are still smiling cheerfully. How then can you utter a sorrowful prayer? By this we can see how important the emotion is to the spirit. Man's expression lies with the emotion, and God's expression is carried out mainly through our emotion. One who is without emotions has no way to express the spirit or God. Thus, one who lives before God and prays must have emotions, even abundant emotions. All who are as cold as ice in their emotion can never be spiritual.

This does not mean that if you have plenty of emotions you are automatically spiritual. It is possible that your abundant emotions will, on the contrary, cause you to become a mess. To be spiritual without becoming a mess, you need an emotion that is moderate, sound, refined, temperate and restrained, tranquil, controlled, spiritual, and abundant. If one would learn all these lessons his emotion would be most useful and precious. It would also become most competent in expressing God as well as expressing the spirit. Such a one is most learned in prayer, and God can be expressed more through him.

By studying church history and reading the biographies of spiritual men, you will find that all spiritual men are full of emotions. The more spiritual a person is, the richer his emotions are. In the Bible there is a weeping prophet by the name of Jeremiah. He said, "mine eye runneth down with water" (Lam. 1:16), and, "mine eye runneth down with rivers of water" (Lam. 3:48). He was really a weeping prophet. The feeling to weep was very heavy in him. But when you read the book of Jeremiah you can sense that, though he wept, his emotion had been disciplined. His sorrowful and weeping emotion had been restricted so that God could come to him and use him to express the sorrowful feelings that were in God's heart. Although God was grieved and hurt because of His people, He had to find someone on this earth who had these feelings. Then when His Spirit came upon that particular one and put those feelings in his spirit, he would then express the sorrowful feeling of God out of his emotion. If Jeremiah had been a merry and cheerful prophet, God would not have been able to use him. Hence, in order that God may be fully expressed through you, you need a spiritual emotion.

X. THE EMOTION AND PRAYER

From the above nine points we can see that only when the emotion has been exercised to the extent that it can be employed by the spirit can it be useful in prayer. Leviticus 10:6-9 mentions that when Aaron's sons, Nadab and Abihu, offered strange fire and died before God, Moses told Aaron and his other two sons, "Uncover not your heads neither rend your clothes," and thus prohibited them from expressing any emotion whatever. And they did according to the word of Moses. If at that time Aaron had wept or uncovered his head, he would not have been able to be the high priest anymore. This is not an easy matter. Aaron was not without grief, but he needed to control his emotion to the extent that he could be useful to God.

XI. THE EMOTION OF PRAYER

If one's emotion has been adjusted to the extent of the above ten points, his emotion is one that can cooperate with God. When the emotion has been exercised to such an extent, then he can be a man of prayer before God.

CHAPTER EIGHT

THE WILL AND PRAYER

I. THE POSITION OF THE WILL

The will is also a part of the soul. We have already covered the matter concerning the mind and the emotion of the soul. With the mind, the emphasis is on the comprehension and understanding of the soul concerning matters or things; with the emotion, the emphasis is on the likes and dislikes of the soul, and with the will, the emphasis is on the decisions and determinations of the soul. For example, with regard to a certain matter or thing, whether or not you decide to have it, to choose it, or to refuse it, these judgments and decisions are the functions of the will. Although the mind occupies a very great part of the soul, it is not the governing organ. The governing organ, the presiding part of the soul, is the will. Determining whether one likes a certain thing or not is the function of one's emotion. His comprehension concerning a certain matter and his understanding regarding a certain thing are the faculties of his mind. Having comprehended and understood it, he likes or dislikes it, but will he choose it or refuse it? This will be decided by the will. Hence, the final deciding organ is the will. In a proper man, the will should rank higher than the mind and the emotion. It should stand in the highest place.

In a normal situation, a man would use his mind to understand and comprehend and his emotion to desire or hate, but the final deciding and determining function belongs to the will. Let us consider someone who comes to listen to the gospel. The first organ he uses is the mind. He listens, understands, and comprehends with his mind. Having understood and comprehended, he uses the next organ, which is the emotion. After his mind is touched, the Holy Spirit penetrating through his mind touches his conscience. Once his conscience is in operation, his emotion is influenced and he wants to believe in the Lord. Thus, he feels sorry about his past life, and his heart begins to incline toward God. At that moment, he needs to exercise his will to decide and determine to believe in the Lord. Hence, it is the will that presides in man. It serves as the presiding organ and decides matters. Although his mind understands something, and his emotion likes it, he is helpless if his will does not choose it. The will is the final deciding organ.

There are many people who act as if they do not have a will. There are also many who act as if they do not use their will. They put their will in subjection to their emotion and also allow it to be obliterated by their mind. Such men are not proper. One who is without a will or who does not use his will is just like a ship without a rudder. Suppose a ship has no rudder or does not use the one it has. That ship will go wherever the wind blows and will thus be without direction. People who act entirely according to the impulse of their emotion, without any control, are just like a ship without a rudder or a car without a brake. This is very dangerous.

The will should be the controlling organ in our soul. The reason someone loses his temper in a fierce way or commits a crime is because his emotion is too active while his will lacks the controlling power. The reason that someone can become so exhilarated he is beside himself and goes beyond the bounds of a normal behavior is also due to the lack of a controlling will. The prayer life of such a one fluctuates with the blowing of the wind. When there is some kind of atmosphere carrying him, he prays; otherwise, he does not pray. His will does not have the controlling strength. This is true both with his personal prayers and his prayers in the meetings. When his emotion is aroused, he will just pray his own prayers according to his own feelings with no concern for the flow of the meeting. However, if his emotion is not aroused, he will not pray at all. Both his public and private prayer life are altogether subject to the stirrings of his emotion and are not under the control of his will. This kind of person cannot be a man of prayer.

The will, subject to the control of the spirit, should be the presiding part of the soul. This is the position of the will.

II. A STRONG WILL

Man's will needs to be strong. The emotion should be soft, but the will should not. To have a soft will is equivalent to having no will. Please consider: if the brake is soft, how can you stop the car? If the rudder of a ship is made of paper, it cannot function as a rudder. It is imperative that the rudder be hard and strong. Likewise, one's will cannot effectively function as a will unless it is strong.

Anyone who follows the Lord faithfully and maintains his standing unchanged till death is a person with a strong will. Every martyr is a man with a firm, strong will. Consider Martin Luther or John Wycliffe. They were people with a strong, resolute will. Again, look at the three friends of Daniel. The trial of the fiery furnace showed that they truly had strong, firm wills. Similarly, our prayer cannot last long unless we have a strong, firm will. The Lord Jesus said, "Watch and pray; pray always." We need a strong, firm will in order to be able to watch and be constant in prayer. One who is a jellyfish can never be watchful. He can only pray sometimes. He cannot endure in prayer. Although prayer is a refined matter, it requires a resolute will. From the first day that Daniel prayed for his people, his words were heard by God, and God sent an angel to answer his prayer. However, the angel met the resistance of an evil prince in the air and fought for three weeks before he could get to the earth. During that time, Daniel, who was on earth, needed a resolute will to persist in prayer for the three weeks. None of those who know how to pray properly and constantly have a weak will. Rather, each one has a will that is strong.

Fallen people have many abnormal conditions such as: the will needs to be strong, yet it is not; the mind needs to be sober, yet it is not; and the emotion needs to be in abundance, yet it is not. But with a spiritual man, his mind is sober and rich; his emotion is certainly abundant and moderate, and his will is definitely strong and firm. We often say that one needs to be bold. But one who has a weak will can never be bold. All the bold ones are men who have a strong will. The three friends of Daniel were really bold when they were there by the furnace, because their wills were really strong. That boldness came from the strength of their will. Some are very weak and can be easily frightened by one little threatening word. Because their will is not resolute, they become afraid. Such a man cannot pray. Satan will use all kinds of methods to torture, destroy, and obliterate the life of prayer that is in man. Therefore, unless man has a strong will, his prayer life will be torn down. Hence, it is necessary to have a strong will in order to maintain the prayer life.

III. A PLIABLE WILL

To be strong is one thing, but to be pliable is another thing. To be strong yet not pliable is to be stubborn. To be strong is proper, but to be stubborn is not proper. Everyone who learns how to pray should have a will that is strong but not stubborn. The will should be pliable. This pliability can be illustrated by the spring in a watch. You may say that the spring is hard, but you may also say that it is pliable. Because the spring is strong yet pliable, it can serve as a motivating power.

To be strong means that I reject everything that is negative. To be pliable means that I receive and yield myself to everything that is positive. I exercise a strong will to deal with everything that is from Satan, but I exercise a pliable will to receive everything that is from God. In our prayers, many times when we have barely touched the presence of God we soon lose it. The main reason is that we are not pliable enough. In our prayer, God's feeling has taken a turn, yet we do not turn. We insist on praying as before. To have such an insistence is not to be properly strong, but to be headstrong.

The day that Peter went up on the housetop to pray and saw the vision of the great sheet, his will was firm but not stubborn—it was pliable. The record in Acts 10 says that when he was praying, he became hungry. Then he saw a certain vessel descending, as it were, a great sheet, wherein were all manner of four-footed beasts, creeping things of the earth, and birds of the heaven. And there came a voice to him, saying, "Rise, Peter; kill, and eat" (v. 13). But Peter said, "Not so, Lord; for I have never eaten any thing that is common or unclean" (v. 14). This shows his resoluteness. But God spoke to him three times, and, during the last time, some men were calling for him at the gate. The Spirit told him to go down to meet them. Once he went down, his attitude was changed and he immediately agreed to go with those Gentiles. Here you can see that Peter's will was very pliable and not stubborn. To be stubborn means to be hard. If he had insisted that regardless of anything he would not communicate with the Gentiles or touch anything that is common and unclean, he would have been a stubborn, hard person.

Many times we are unable to follow the move of the Spirit in our prayers, for we are strong to the extent that we become hard. This is a very great problem of ours. The problem arises, not only with regard to prayer, but in many other matters, also. Sometimes when we need to be strong, we are not. At other times, in being strong, we go too far and become hard. Hence, we cannot see the light, touch the presence of God, or have spiritual growth. At the same time, we are not able to endure in prayer. The firmness of our will needs the corresponding pliability. The pliability must balance the firmness if the will is suitable for prayer. Satan always utilizes men, things, and outside activities to consume, extinguish, and obliterate our prayer life. Hence, we need to exercise our will in order to stand fast. At the same time, in our prayers, our will should at all times be able to submit and turn according to the consciousness in our spirit.

Consider how soft the spring in a clock or watch is. Yet once it has been wound and starts to move the hands of the clock, it will not yield or be subdued—that is its firmness. Once they have been disturbed by some trivial matter, some are not able to pray. This shows that their will is not firm enough. On the other hand, there are some who are very strong, and who insist on praying for a certain matter. They do not know how to turn and follow the move of the Spirit in them. This shows that they are not pliable enough. Many have a will that is either too soft or too hard. But neither softness nor hardness is desirable. The kind of will we need is one that is strong yet not hard, and pliable yet not soft.

IV. THE RULING OF THE WILL

The ruling of the will means that the will is in control. It is not the will that is being ruled; rather, it is the will that is ruling, controlling the other parts of the soul. In the chapter concerning the emotion we said that the emotion should be controlled by the will. That day when the two sons of Aaron violated the holiness of God and were struck dead, Aaron did not weep. If he had not exercised his will he would surely have wailed and wept bitterly. But because he exercised his will to rule over his emotion, he was able to completely obey Moses' word and show no sign of mourning. That was not an easy thing to do. The will cannot rule in this way unless it has been exercised to the extent that its firmness and pliability are in full cooperation with one another.

Ephesians 4 tells us, "Be angry, and do not sin" (v. 26). Being angry is a matter of the emotion, but to sin not is a matter of the ruling of the will. The verse goes on to say, "do not let the sun go down on your indignation." Once the sun sets, your anger has to disappear with it. The question is, how can you dispel your anger? This can only be done through the controlling of the will. But with some, once they are angry their anger remains; once they are offended by others they will not forgive them during their entire lifetime. Please remember, such a situation indicates that the will is not in control. The will is not able to rule over the emotion. To be a good Christian who is able to pray, one's will must be able to dominate the emotion. Regardless how much a brother has provoked you to anger, your anger must be dispelled with the going down of the sun. One whose will has been exercised and subjected to the rule of the spirit is able to be angry for one minute and to dispel his anger the next.

I have heard it said, "This person or that thing has made me so angry that I cannot pray anymore." It is true that you cannot pray if you are angry. If you want to pray, you need to dispel your anger. But in order to dissipate your anger, you need your will to rule over your emotion. It is possible that a brother really has done something wrong which made you angry. But please remember, a half minute later your anger should cool down. Otherwise you will not be able to pray.

It is not only anger that makes one unable to pray. Even joy can prevent one from praying. Someone may be so excited over his son's passing an examination for studying abroad that he cannot pray. He really wants to give thanks to God, but because he cannot pray he has no way to give thanks. This proves that his will is not in control.

In the normal condition, neither happiness nor anger will render you unable to pray. Rather, when it is time to pray, your will is able to apply the brake to your emotion. At such a time, the qualities of the emotion will demonstrate soundness, tranquility, temperance, and restraint, because the emotion is being regulated by the will. Unless the will has been adjusted properly, the emotion will never be normal, because they are connected to one another. Someone may ask, "Why do you bring out these complicated matters when speaking of prayer?" Keep in mind that prayer involves human beings performing a task, and within this human machine there are many complicated things. If there is something wrong with any part of a car, the car cannot be driven and will require some repair work. In like manner, if any part within you goes wrong, you will not be able to pray. Hence, to pray competently, the parts of one's being need to be proper.

The will not only needs to control the emotion; it also needs to control the mind. Some always have vain imaginations in their mind. The moment they kneel down to pray their mind begins to travel around the world. In less than two or three minutes they may have circled around the world twice. This shows that they have not practiced using their will to control their mind. You may say, "This is the disobedience of my mind." Whether your mind is obedient or disobedient is another matter. You still need to exercise your will. It is imperative that your will be the ruling organ in your being. It should not follow that you would hit someone simply because you are angry now. This cannot be. It is the will, not the emotion, that should rule. Neither should you go ahead with a certain matter simply because your mind is clear

about it. Even when you are clear, you should still wait for the
will to make a decision before you make a move to do anything. It is the will, not the mind, that should rule.

A ship is secure if it can depend on its rudder to determine
its direction. If a car can depend on its brakes to control its
speed, that car is definitely safe. But if the direction of the
ship is not determined by its rudder, and the speed of the car
is not controlled by its brakes, both the ship and the car are
very dangerous. Likewise, in both our walk and our prayer we
must allow our will to rule over our emotion and mind. Thus,
we can be proper humans. To behave according to an undisci-
plined mind and emotion is dangerous. A child who always
plays but is not willing to study surely has a weak will. If his
will is strong and is being used properly, it will restrict him
from playing when he should be studying. Therefore, learn to
exercise the will so that it will be strong yet pliable. Learn
also to allow the will to rule, to take the lead, controlling the
mind and the emotion. Thus, you can be a proper man. When
this condition exists, you can pray.

V. THE RELATIONSHIP BETWEEN THE WILL
AND THE SPIRIT

The function of the mind is to understand the consciousness in the spirit. The function of the emotion is to enable the
spirit to be expressed. But without the decision of the will,
even though the mind has understood something and the
emotion is able to express it, such understanding and expression are useless. For example, your mind has understood that
the sense within your spirit is directing you to pray. Your
emotion is also able to express the feeling of the spirit. However, your will is not taking a stand or making a decision. In
such a case you are still unable to pray. Let us illustrate in
this way: suppose that at the Lord's table someone really has
an inspiration. His mind understands the inspiration as
being a sense of the Lord's glory. His emotion really feels the
Lord's glory to the extent that the joy almost moves him to
tears. But at this time he remains indecisive and is not willing to pray because of various considerations. Why is this so?
This shows a lack in the will. The will is not cooperating with

the spirit. While he is considering this and thinking about that, another brother calls out a hymn. Following the singing of the hymn he is still hesitating. In the meantime, another brother offers a prayer. Thus his indecisiveness has quenched his inspiration. After the meeting he goes home and is restless the whole night. He definitely had an inspiration, but it was not expressed. It was not because his mind was not able to understand it; neither was it because he did not have the emotion to express it. It was simply because his will was not decisive enough to execute it. Since his will was weak and unable to make a decision, he became timid. He should have exercised his will to immediately make a decision and burst forth with a prayer. Then that which was in his spirit would have been released. This is the function of the will in relation to the spirit.

VI. THE WILL AND PRAYER

Unless one has a sober mind and a moderate emotion, he cannot pray effective prayers. Similarly, unless one has a strong yet pliable will, he is unable to pray properly. Hence, there is a very close relationship between the will and prayer. Every spiritual matter, no matter what it is, requires the proper exercise of the will. The same applies even to the time when one initially is stirred to believe in the Lord. Someone may be touched in the gospel preaching meeting and may even be weeping. But if you ask him to stand up and receive the Lord, he may refuse to make a decision with his will. He may say that he will think it over, or that he will go home to talk it over with his wife, etc. He has understood and is touched. Both his mind and his emotion are in function. But since he refuses to use his will, there is no way for him to be saved. The same principle operates in the relationship between the will and prayer. It is absolutely necessary to exercise the will properly in order to pray effectively.

VII. THE PRAYER OF THE WILL

We often think that prayer is a matter entirely related to the spirit. This is correct. But, many times there is no inspiration. Shall we then give up praying? No. In such times you must learn to pray with your will first. By praying with the will first, you can easily usher in the inspiration. It is like driving a car. The initial step is not to apply the gas but to turn on the ignition. Once the ignition is on, it immediately causes the combustion of the gasoline. Many times you may want to pray, yet your spirit is unmoved. If you keep waiting until your spirit is moved, you may not pray for the entire day. Suppose as you rise in the morning your spirit is unmoved, so you do not pray. After waiting for two hours there is still no movement in your spirit, and you still do not pray. Today there is no inspiration, so there is no prayer. Tomorrow there is still no inspiration, so there is still no prayer. Perhaps for one whole week there is no inspiration and, therefore, no prayer. It is very dangerous to keep on waiting until you are moved in your spirit in order to pray. Hence, you need to learn to pray with your will in order to usher in the inspiration.

The same situation may occur in the meetings. Yes, when we meet together we should wait for inspiration and pray by inspiration. But many times it is not right, especially for some brothers who are in a leading position to help the meeting, to simply sit there, stiffly and passively, waiting for the so-called inspiration. Sometimes there is the inspiration, so that there is no need for you to take the initiative. The Holy Spirit is initiating, and all you need to do is pray according to the Spirit. But there are other times when there is no clear indication of the Spirit's initiation. Of course you must first be purified, forgiven, looking to the Lord, and in fellowship with Him. Then, when you know there is a need to pray in the meeting, you should exercise your will to release the meeting. Once you exercise your will to open your mouth and pray, in less than two sentences you can cause your spirit to rise up. On some special occasion a brother might be asked to offer a prayer. He may not have any inspiration at that particular moment, but since he was asked, he would have to exercise his will and pray. If he is one who fears God, has fellowship with Him, has his spirit exercised, and has touched the spirit, in less than three to five sentences his spirit comes into function. This prayer of his will, like turning the ignition on when driving a car, immediately activates the spirit, causing it to rise up. This is called the prayer of the will.

Furthermore, sometimes it seems that while praying, your inspiration has been interrupted, yet you feel you have not discharged the burden of your prayer. At such a time you need to sustain that prayer with your will. After sustaining it for one or two minutes you will see that the inspiration returns. The will is a very useful faculty. Whenever the spirit falls short you need to fill in with the will. Learn to exercise your will in cooperation with your spirit, but do not use your will apart from the spirit. The function of the will is to cooperate with the spirit and to fill in for the spirit. Before the spirit is stirred up you may start with your will. While the spirit seems to be resting you should also fill in with your will. These initiating or filling-in prayers are called the prayers of the will.

Furthermore, when the Bible says "pray," "be watchful," "pray always," "pray in spirit," etc., these imperatives are commands directed at our will. All require the function of the will. Only the functioning of the will can maintain the life of prayer.

Daniel 9:2-3 says, "I Daniel understood by books the number of the years, whereof the word of the LORD came to Jeremiah the prophet, that he would accomplish seventy years in the desolations of Jerusalem. And I set my face unto the Lord God, to seek by prayer and supplications, with fasting, and sackcloth, and ashes." This shows that Daniel's prayer was altogether an action of his will. His prayer was not initiated by the spirit but by the will. But when you proceed to read the words after Daniel 9:3, you will notice that, although in the beginning it was Daniel who set himself to pray according to his will, after a few sentences his spirit was stirred up. When you read the prayer in Daniel, chapter nine, you can realize that it was entirely in the spirit. With his will he initiated that prayer and moved his spirit—he substituted his will in the place of his spirit, and he used his will to set his spirit on fire. Hence, we see the will is extremely important to prayer. The will not only has to move the spirit to pray, but if necessary, it has to pray in place of the spirit. This is the prayer of the will.

CHAPTER NINE

THE CONSCIENCE AND PRAYER

I. THE POSITION OF THE CONSCIENCE

The conscience is the most evident part of the human spirit. The human spirit also contains two other parts, the intuition and the fellowship. Within a fallen man the latter two faculties are usually obscure. The conscience, however, is still able to manifest its function, but only to a small degree. In those who are saved, both the intuition and the fellowship have resumed their respective functions. However, the most distinct function of the spirit still lies with the conscience. As the conscience is the most manifest part, so it is also the most important part of the spirit. In the chapter on the spirit of prayer, we stated that a man who wishes to pray must be in spirit and that his spirit must be well-exercised. But to exercise his spirit, he must first exercise his conscience. Unless a man's conscience has been properly dealt with, his spirit will surely become ineffective before God. If the conscience is improper, the spirit becomes out of function and deflated. Hence, we see what an important position the conscience has within us.

Although the conscience is a major part of our spirit, it is not our ego. Our personality, our ego, is the soul. The soul with its various faculties is the ruling factor of our actions— our thinking, feeling, and deciding. As far as our actions are concerned, the ruling factor is the soul with its various organs not the conscience. Figuratively speaking, the conscience is equivalent to the Control Yuan (one of the five major branches of the Chinese government) while the various parts of the soul are like the Legislative Yuan. It is the responsibility of the conscience to regulate all the activities of the soul. The conscience does not advocate, comprehend, or desire. It regulates, or oversees. Whether you do something right or wrong; whether you are acceptable to God or not; whether your thinking is in darkness or in the light; whether your emotion is proper or improper; and whether your judgment is pleasing to God or not—all these are under the supervision and inspection of the conscience. If your thought is acceptable to God, the conscience will say yes; otherwise, it will say no. If your preference is pleasing to God, it will approve; if not, it will disapprove. If your decision or choice is agreeable to Him, it will say amen; otherwise, it will raise an objection.

The above points constitute the position of the conscience. The conscience is the major part, the most evident part of the spirit. And although it is not the commanding organ of the ego, it is the organ that supervises and checks the various parts of the soul.

II. A GOOD CONSCIENCE

First Timothy 1:5 and 19 speak of a good conscience. In our understanding, a good conscience is a conscience void of offense. But there is a difference between being good, and being void of offense. In this point we shall cover the matter of a good conscience, and in the following point will look into the matter of a conscience void of offense.

Among the Chinese, some have the saying, "So-and-so's conscience is bad," or "So-and-so's conscience is very good." This thought about a good conscience or a bad conscience really fits in with the concept of the New Testament. In the New Testament, a good conscience denotes a conscience that is not crooked or perverted, but very normal and right. Not to be perverted is to be normal, while not to be crooked is to be right. A good conscience is one that is very normal and right. On the contrary, a bad conscience is one that is perverted and crooked. Suppose it is quite evident that I have stolen my employer's money, yet I justify my action by saying that he owes me the money. I may reason that since my employer does not pay me what I should earn, it is therefore right for me to steal from him in some way to make up the difference.

Everyone knows that this kind of reasoning is called twisting the facts. If I can reason this way, it proves that my conscience is bad.

In 1 Timothy chapter one, the apostle says that some, having thrust their conscience from them, suffered shipwreck concerning the faith. Hence, a Christian must continually exercise himself to have a conscience that is right and normal, not crooked or perverted. He should be fair and just. If yes, say yes. If no, say no; if you are wrong, admit it; if you are right, avow it even at the cost of your head—not fearing opposition or difficulty. If you make a mistake, confess it, even though you may suffer loss. Maintain this attitude in dealing with yourself and with others. Brothers and sisters often demonstrate an improper conscience. For example, if a matter involves someone's wife or relatives, his words will be entirely different than if it involves someone else. If others are at fault, he will readily criticize and condemn. But if his younger brother is at fault, he will play it down, make light of it, and even look for an excuse to whitewash it or cover it up. Such behavior shows that the conscience is improper, abnormal, and crooked. It is a bad conscience. If we wish to serve before God and be a praying one, our conscience must be upright. If my wife or my younger brother or even I myself am at fault, I must condemn the mistake. Draw a very straight line and be very upright so that, regardless of who, what, where or when, if any action crosses the line, it is judged wrong. This is an impartial conscience, a good conscience.

When the apostle Paul wrote the two letters to Timothy the church was in a very degraded condition, and many things were in darkness. At that particular time, the apostle especially spoke about the conscience. At such an hour, speaking from the human standpoint, to pass judgment on anything would require one to consider the conscience as the standard. Debating, arguing, and disputing are useless. You just need to check with your conscience.

When I lived in north China over thirty years ago, I always encountered outside opposition with regard to the truths and messages I preached. Following the release of every message given on the Lord's day or in the conference meetings, the reactions always came quickly. Some brother would come and tell me, "Brother Lee, a certain elder, or pastor, or preacher said that your teaching is wrong and that you preach heresy." Sometimes I would just say this: "If only he would allow the Lord Jesus to touch every one of his possessions, he would know that my teaching is right." You know what I mean. Why did he say this particular message of mine was wrong? Because his conscience was not upright, and that particular message happened to touch the matter of his possessions before the Lord. If he was one who lived absolutely for the Lord and was fully consecrated, he would surely have an upright conscience. If he spoke according to an upright conscience, he would have to admit that the message I gave was right. But since he was in a state of desolation and failure before the Lord, his conscience became twisted, distorting the facts, and he defended himself. Consequently, he was not able to speak according to an upright conscience.

The most accurate part within a man is his conscience. But when man is in a fallen, darkened state, the darkness and degradation will influence his conscience, causing it to be warped. When the church is entirely in the light and walking according to the truth, there is no problem. But when the church is degraded and fallen, resulting in confusion, preaching the truth will not be very profitable. For if the conscience is confused and one is distant from the Lord, how can he contend for the truth? It was in such a situation that the apostle wrote the epistles to Timothy, especially pointing out the matter of conscience. People have often come to argue with us concerning a certain truth. At the end of every argument we just said, "Brother, since we are in a dark age today, every child of God must live before the Lord by his own conscience." The moment we said that, such a person would not argue with us anymore. The moment we touched his conscience, he did not have much to say. For regardless of the circumstances, there is always a standard in man's conscience. However, man usually does not maintain a sufficiently good conscience. Rather, he often goes against his conscience and bends it, thus producing a bad conscience. During the church's degradation you and I need to exercise ourselves not to follow this crooked age or walk according to the degraded condition of Christianity. Rather, we must maintain an upright, normal, proper, and good conscience. Thus, we can be a proper man of prayer.

III. A CONSCIENCE VOID OF OFFENSE— A GUILTLESS CONSCIENCE

A conscience void of offense is a guiltless conscience. To be guiltless means that all wrongdoings which were condemned by the conscience have been dealt with before God and have been forgiven by Him. Hence, there is no more feeling of guilt and condemnation in the conscience. This is expressed in Acts 24:16 in these words: "And herein do I exercise myself, to have always a conscience void of offense toward God, and toward men." Once you make an error, you should always deal with it immediately so that there will be no offense, guilt, or blemish on your conscience. Your conscience should be free from condemnation before God as well as free from accusation before men. Your conscience should respond clearly when it is touched.

Brothers, this is a very serious matter. You may be able to fool everyone else, but please remember, you can never fool your conscience. Especially in times of the church's degradation and confusion, many people like to debate about doctrines and dispute over matters of service to God. If you have a conscience void of offense and have thoroughly dealt with everything before God, then when you argue with others there will be a clear, confirming response within you. But suppose you did not obey the light you saw, or you did not answer a certain demand of God, or you were unwilling to forsake something as God required. Then there would be an offense in your conscience, and you would not be able to speak words that carry weight and which evoke a clear, confirming response within.

In the past years we have met many people who were like this. Sometimes we ourselves are the same because our unwillingness to answer a certain demand of God causes an offense in our conscience. This offense becomes a leak within us. And even though we sing and minister, our spirit is not strong, neither do our prayers and words have a clear sound. Then one day, by the grace of God, we deal with the particular offense and answer God's demand. Immediately the offense in our conscience is gone, the sound of our prayer is changed, and when we stand up again to give a testimony, there is an inner confirmation which is a conscience void of offense.

Today, during the church's degradation, it is not easy for one who serves God to keep his conscience free from offense. Paul spoke such a word while he was being judged. At that time not only the worldly power was resisting him, but the authorities of Judaism were continuously condemning him with the Word of God and the laws of the Old Testament. It was not an easy thing for Paul to keep a conscience void of offense before God. He was able to stand before the Gentile officials and the Jewish rulers, that is, both the political and religious groups, and say with a loud voice, "And herein do I exercise myself, to have always a conscience void of offense toward God, and toward men." As far as politics are concerned, he was innocent; and as far as religion, that is, the laws of Judaism, is concerned, he was faultless. His conscience before God was solid, not hollow. There was no leak, hole, offense, guilt, sin, or accusation in his conscience. He was able to stand before both groups and speak clearly and with weight.

The leaders of the Jewish religion had a guilty conscience before God. If Paul had questioned them, just a light, little prick would have proven that they had a bad conscience. Since Paul's conscience had been dealt with before God, he could say that his conscience was without offense; therefore, he was a man who served God and was also a man of prayer. His conscience was supporting him because there was no flaw in it. By the cleansing of the precious blood, we must keep our conscience free from any offense so that we may be men of prayer.

IV. A CLEAN, PURE CONSCIENCE

The Lord Jesus said, "Blessed are the pure in heart" (Matt. 5:8). This refers not just to a clean heart but to a pure heart. We also need a clean, pure conscience. In 2 Timothy 1:3 the apostle says that he served God with a pure conscience. This is not just a clean conscience. Something that is clean is not necessarily pure, because there may be mixture in it. For instance, if you put a piece of steel and a piece of wood together and give them a thorough washing, they will be clean but not pure. We should have a conscience that is pure as well as clean.

Suppose someone asks God for a number of proper things, but he does not seek God absolutely in his conscience and has no sense of condemnation. This kind of conscience may be clean, but it is not sufficiently pure. A man can be for God and at the same time be for the work of the gospel—to preach the gospel successfully and to work and bring forth fruit. These things are neither bad nor defiled, but the intention within him may not be pure. He may still desire other things besides God. To have fruit in gospel preaching, to have power in carrying on the work, and to have the spreading and increase in leading the church—these are good, but the motive behind them may not be pure. This means the conscience is impure.

What does it mean to have a pure conscience? It means that you can say to God, "God, I only want You and nothing else. I do not even care for the work of the gospel, power for the work, fruits of the work, or the spreading and increase of the church. I just want You." Such a conscience is a pure conscience. During the degradation of the church, Paul spoke in the letters to Timothy concerning a pure conscience as well as a good conscience. He said that he served God with a pure conscience. His conscience only sought God. Anything that was outside God had no place in him. He was one who served God with a conscience that was pure to such an extent.

Some have seriously condemned their work before God. This does not mean that their work was unsuccessful. On the contrary, their work may have been very effective. A good number of people may have been saved, and many may have received help. But one day when the light of God shines upon them, they will say to the Lord, "O Lord, these things have largely replaced You and have robbed You of Your place in me. Within me I am not pure, single, or absolute enough toward You. I still seek things other than You." Such men, when you meet them, will give you a deep sense that they are those who live before God and whose conscience is pure. Please remember, only people like this can work for God, and the real fruit of the work will be manifested through them. But those who care for the results of the work may not always have results. And those who seek power to preach the gospel may not necessarily obtain power. Real results and real power are with those who care only for God Himself, for the results and the power are just God Himself. Such men have a pure conscience within them. Hence, they can serve God.

You need to understand the situation at the time Paul wrote the second epistle to Timothy. If he did not desire God alone, and if his conscience were not fixed on Him alone, it would have been impossible for him to stand firm at that time. For at that time he had lost everything. The churches in Asia, which had received the greatest help from him, had deserted him. Even Demas, his co-worker, having loved the present world, had forsaken him and gone to Thessalonica. All those who were beside him deserted him and left him alone in the prison. He had to handle the matter of his defense by himself. Nevertheless, he was not discouraged, for he knew what his desire was. He desired neither the church nor the work, but only God Himself. Therefore, in spite of the fact that the environment was entirely negative, he remained steadfast. His conscience was not only clean, but also pure.

If our conscience can be pure to such an extent, we also will condemn all things that are outside God. Not only will we condemn those things that are evil, but also those that are good, for we know that those things are not God Himself. What we seek is not the work, the blessings, or the church of God. What we desire is just God Himself. Then our conscience is not only clean but also pure. This is the word used by Paul when writing the second epistle to Timothy. At that time he was not only rejected by the Gentiles, but also was forsaken by the churches and his fellow-workers. Although everyone deserted him, he knew that the Lord had not left him. Hence, in such a trying hour, he was able to say that he served God with a pure conscience.

Brothers and sisters, many times God may not listen to

our prayers. In the beginning, you may pray for ten things and know God has answered every one of them. But gradually you dare not and cannot pray for a number of things because you know that these are not what God is after. You know that He would not listen to your prayer for such things. If you do not deal with your conscience so that it becomes pure, you will say, "Oh, why should I pray? God would not listen to my prayer anyway. I do not need to pray anymore, neither do I need to serve God." But if your conscience is pure to the degree that you do not care for anything but God Himself, then in this circumstance you would not murmur to God. Instead, you would say to Him, "God, I thank and praise You for not answering this particular prayer of mine, because what I asked for at that time was not You Yourself. Although it was something good and was not sinful, it still was not what You want." When your conscience is clean and pure to this extent, you can be a very deep, very proper man of prayer.

Today, many of our prayers are not deep or proper enough. We are like children asking our parents for whatever we want. In the past our parents, considering that we were still young, gave us some things according to what we had asked. The same is true in our experience with the Lord. But gradually, as we grow before the Lord, we can no longer pray as we wish. In some instances we are not able to open our mouth and ask. In other instances, when the Lord fails to answer our prayer, we are no longer able to complain. Rather, we give thanks, for we know that God would never give us those things that are outside Himself. Hence, to be a deeper, proper man of prayer has very much to do with having a pure conscience.

V. THE CLEANSING OF THE CONSCIENCE

Regardless how much we exercise ourselves to have a good and pure conscience, we still need to cleanse our conscience daily. This is because we are still in the old creation, in the flesh, and in this evil, defiled age. We simply do not know how many times in a single day we have been contaminated and have committed offenses. The defilement and guilt in our conscience can only be washed by the blood of Jesus. This is according to Hebrews 10:22, "having our hearts sprinkled from an evil conscience."

The more one prays before God, the more he realizes the necessity of the blood. The realization of our need for the blood is entirely a sense in our conscience. If you do not live much before God or pray much, you will not be able to sense the urgency of the blood. It is when you really live before God that the words in 1 John 1:7-9 will be effectually fulfilled in you. God is light. The more you are in the light, the more you will realize that you have offended a certain person, or that you are wrong in a certain matter. You will also realize that you were defiled when you contacted someone, and you will feel guilty about certain motives and thoughts. You will have all sorts of accusations in your conscience. All these are the offenses of the conscience. At such a time, unless you apply the blood, your conscience will become defiled. The more one prays, draws near to God, and lives in prayer and fellowship, the more he will sense the absolute necessity of the blood. He will be one who always experiences the cleansing of the blood.

Every time a man goes before God, he invariably has to pass through the altar and the blood. According to the type in the Old Testament, everyone who intends to go into the Holy of Holies to draw near to God must first offer the sacrifice and shed the blood at the altar. Then he can bring the blood of the sin offering with him into the Holy of Holies and sprinkle it before God. This means that every time you go before God to pray, your conscience needs to be cleansed by the blood. While we are still in this flesh and in this age, no one can go before God to pray at any time without applying the blood. If, instead of applying the blood, you trust in your own goodness, your conscience will not be able to bear witness with you. There will always be some defilement or guilt in you, and you will always be at fault or not faithful enough in some matter. If you are just a little negligent, there will be the accusation in your conscience, and this accusation will become an offense. Therefore, if you wish to remove the offense in your conscience, you must continually seek the cleansing of the blood.

VI. THE CONSCIENCE AND PRAYER

Hebrews 10:22, 2 Timothy 1:3, and Acts 23:1 show us that the conscience is absolutely related to prayer. One whose conscience is not cleansed cannot pray because there is a separation between him and God. One whose conscience is not pure enough also cannot pray before God. Once there is an accusation or a condemnation in your conscience, you will sense immediately that there is a curtain and a veil as well, in you. The curtain creates a distance, a separation between you and God; whereas the veil puts a cover over you so that you are unable to see God. Not only so, but once the conscience has a problem, it will be difficult to have faith. Once there is a hole in the conscience, faith leaks out. When the conscience is bad, has offense, is not pure enough, or is not being cleansed by the precious blood, one cannot pray before God. You may pray hastily, but you always feel that you are praying outside the curtain and have not entered into the Holy of Holies. Also, you always feel that there is a veil covering your heart. Thus, you cannot see the light of God's face and you are not in His presence. Your prayer is not getting through to God. It seems that there is a wall of separation or a layer of covering which hinders your prayer from reaching God. Hence, in order to have good, proper prayers, prayers that reach God, you need to deal with your conscience until it becomes good, void of offense, pure, and cleansed. Then, as there is no more condemnation in your conscience, you will be able to pray. Hence, there is an absolute relationship between the conscience and prayer.

VII. THE CONSCIENCE FOR PRAYER

Summing up the previous few points we can see that a conscience for prayer is a good conscience, a conscience void of offense and guilt, a conscience free from accusation. It is also a clean, pure conscience, and a conscience that is always being cleansed by the precious blood. Having such a conscience, when you enter into God's presence and pray, you will sense that you are before Him, in the light of His face, and without either a separating curtain or a covering veil.

Whenever you go before God to pray you ought to deal with your conscience in a proper, detailed way. After dealing in this way, you can come boldly and pray to God out of a clean, pure conscience—a conscience void of offense, a good conscience. You know that you have passed through the curtain so there is no separation between you and God. You also know that there is no veil, no covering in you. You are in God's presence, in the light of His face, and there is a free-flowing communion between you and God. At that moment your conscience will enable you to pray boldly, powerfully, and confidently. Your conscience will confirm and support your prayer. Moreover, as there is such a free flow and mingling between you and God, God is able to anoint you with His heart's desire. Consequently, His desire becomes your desire and His feeling becomes your feeling. He prays in you, and you pray with Him. Therefore, if we wish to pray, we need to have a conscience that will enable us to pray.

CHAPTER TEN

THE HEART FOR PRAYER

I. THE POSITION OF THE HEART

The Bible clearly shows us that man was created with three parts: the spirit, the soul, and the body. The outermost part of man is the body; the innermost part is the spirit. Between these two is the soul. We have said that the spirit is composed of the conscience, the fellowship, and the intuition. We have also said that the soul is composed of the mind, the emotion, and the will. But the Scriptures show us that there is another important organ in man—the heart. The heart is composed of elements from both the soul and the spirit. It includes one part of the spirit and all the parts of the soul.

The mind, emotion, and will of the soul, and the conscience of the spirit, each constitutes a part of the heart. For example, speaking of the mind, Hebrews 4:12 says, "the thoughts...of the heart." The heart being capable of having thoughts clearly indicates that the mind, a part of the soul, is also a part of the heart. Hebrews 4:12 also speaks of the "intents of the heart." While the thoughts are something of the mind, the intents are something of the will. Thus we can see plainly that both the mind and the will are parts of the heart. Furthermore, John 16:22 says, "your heart will rejoice" and 14:1 says, "Let not your heart be troubled." Since to rejoice and to be troubled are something of the emotion, the heart also includes the emotion. Therefore, it is clear that the three parts of the soul are all constituents of the heart.

Moreover, Hebrews 10:22 says, "our hearts sprinkled from an evil conscience." Also, 1 John 3:20 mentions that our heart condemns us. Condemnation is a function of the conscience. Hence, we know that the heart also includes the conscience.

In summary, the heart is composed of four parts: the mind, the will, the emotion, and the conscience. The mind, will, and emotion are the elements of the soul, and the conscience is a major part of the spirit. If we were to realize the component parts of our heart, we would immediately be aware of its position. The position of the heart encompasses the mind, will, emotion, and conscience; it is a very broad position which includes all the parts of the soul plus a major part of the spirit. Thus, the heart is the most comprehensive part in our whole being.

II. A TRUE HEART

Speaking of the heart, the Bible pays attention first to its truthfulness. Hebrews 10:22 tells us that the heart needs to be true. All those who come before God should have a true heart. Here, to be true means to be genuine and upright, not false or crooked. The heart of an insincere man is surely not true. Not only so, to be true also means to be single-minded. If a person comes before God to seek something in addition to God, he is double-minded, and his heart is not true. A true heart is real and not false, right and not bent, single and not double. It desires only one thing—God Himself.

When one comes to pray to God, he should only desire God Himself. He should desire nothing outside God. He should only seek God's will and not anything that is outside His will. Many times when one comes to pray to God for a certain thing, he will ask God to show him His heart's desire, but he has his own desire also. Such a heart is false, doubting, and untrue. The heart needs to be single, seeking only God's desire. It is of foremost importance that the heart be true before God.

III. A PURE HEART

Matthew 5:8 says, "Blessed are the pure in heart, for they shall see God." Psalm 73:1 says, "Truly God is good to Israel, even to such as are of a clean heart." A pure heart is more than just a clean heart. It is a heart that simply wants God

Himself and has no aim or goal other than God Himself. Hence, Matthew 5:8 says, "Blessed are the pure in heart, for they shall see God." What they desire within is God Himself, so it follows that what they see is also God Himself. Hence, speaking of a pure heart, the emphasis is not that the heart should be free from evil or defiled thoughts, but that it should want God alone. The heart singly and purely wants God Himself and His heart's desire.

Please remember, a heart that is not upright or single is an untrue heart. But many times our heart seems to be true, yet it is impure because it still desires numerous things besides God. Our heart appears to be true before men, yet it is still untrue in God's eyes because we are not pure and single within. To be true one needs to be pure, and to be pure one also needs to be true. In the end we see that these two points show us that our heart should just want God alone. If it desires anything other than God, it has a problem concerning being single and pure. If our heart remains two-sided and impure before God, we will have great difficulty in prayer. Hence, in order to learn how to pray, we must deal with the matter of the heart.

IV. A HEART WITHOUT CONDEMNATION

First John 3:20-21 speaks of the condemnation of the heart. It says that God is greater than our heart, and if our heart condemns us, God will condemn us even more. But if our heart does not condemn us, we have boldness toward God. The part of our heart that condemns us is the conscience. The condemnation in the heart is the function of the conscience. A heart without condemnation is a heart in which there is no offense or fault in the conscience. If we want to learn how to pray, we must deal with our heart until it is free from condemnation.

To pray to God, the heart needs to have boldness, which results from having no barrier between it and God. Once the heart loses its boldness due to condemnation, prayer will become very difficult. Not only will it be difficult to have faith after prayer, it will even be very hard to have faith while praying. If the heart condemns itself, God will condemn you even more. Then you will have no way to pray. Hence, in order to pray, you need to deal with your heart until it is absolutely free from condemnation. Then you can go with boldness before God, and your prayer will be answered.

V. A TURNED HEART

Second Corinthians 3:14-16 tells us that to this very day the children of Israel still have a veil lying upon their heart. There remains an opaqueness, a covering, between them and God. But whenever the heart turns to the Lord, the veil is taken away. Their heart turned to things other than the Lord, and that turning away is the veil. So, in order to learn how to pray, the heart must be turned from everything else to the Lord.

In His teaching on the mountain the Lord Jesus said that where your treasure is, there will your heart be also. The heart is like the needle of a compass which points to whatever attracts it. If we love our children more than God, then our heart will point and turn to our children. If we love clothing more than God, then our heart will point toward the clothing. If we love education, position, or money more than God, our heart will spontaneously turn toward those things. And once our heart is turned toward those things, it becomes distracted and many problems appear. It is impure and untrue, and there is no way for it to be free from condemnation. Therefore, we must turn our heart to God. When the heart is turned in the proper direction, completely turned to God, then it can really be without condemnation. If the heart is not turned to God, it can never be free from condemnation. You may be able to deceive others, but you can never deceive God. Neither can you deceive yourself. Hence, you must learn to deal with your heart by turning it to God.

Many times, in the prayer meetings or the Lord's table meetings, there are too few who pray, give thanks, or praise. In all likelihood it is because brothers and sisters have problems with their hearts. If your heart was not proper before God during the past week, when you come to break the bread on the Lord's day, naturally you will not be able to give thanks or offer praise. At the same time it will not be easy to be inspired. Our heart may be just slightly inclined to things other than God. Even such a slight deviation will cause us to sense the presence of a veil between us and God. There will be an opaqueness within, so that we can no longer see God. Actually, it is not that His face is not open; rather, it is we who are covered within. If I took a handkerchief and put it over my face, I would not be able to see you. In reality, it is not that your face is turned away from me, but that my eyes are prevented from seeing you.

Furthermore, even though I may not cover my face, if I turn my back to you, this will become a veil which prevents me from seeing you. Second Corinthians 3:16 says that whenever your heart shall turn to the Lord, the veil shall be taken away. The veil which is spoken of there is the turning of your back to the Lord. When your heart is turned away from God to other things, that turning away becomes a veil which prevents you from seeing God. If your heart is on your children, then your children become your veil. If your heart is on your wealth, then your wealth becomes your veil. If your heart is inclined toward education, then education becomes your veil.

Some have come to me asking, "Brother Lee, why don't I have light when I read the Bible?" I have often answered, "Brother, there is no other reason than that your heart is not set upon God. God is light. As your heart is set upon things other than God, those things become a veil to you. Since your heart loves those things, when you read the Bible, instead of light, the veil comes. Once the veil comes, you have no light."

There are also some who say, "When I pray, it seems there is something between God and me, and I cannot touch Him. What is the reason?" I answer in this way, "I am afraid the main reason is that your heart is inclined to something other than God. If your heart is inclined toward other things, how can you see the light of His face? It is impossible."

When the children of Israel were at the foot of Mount Sinai, they had a veil upon them because they were not singly and purely after God, but were after other things. If our heart loves our children, wealth, or clothing more than God, these things become a veil. But also, even if our heart loves gospel preaching or the work more than God, that gospel preaching

and that work will become a veil. It is very difficult for some
Christians to see light because they pay more attention to
God's work than to God Himself. They allow the work to
replace God. It seems they maintain the attitude that they
can sacrifice God, but not the work. They can let go of God's
will and His desire, but they must keep the work at all costs.
Please remember, even such a work can become a veil, and
cause them to have no light within. Their lack of light is not
because God does not shine on them, but because the veil is
there. Their heart is not pointing toward God Himself, but to
things other than God.

If we wish to learn how to pray and draw near to God, we
must set our heart right and turn it to God. Not only do I not
love the world, sin, fashion, and money, but even God's work
cannot attract me—for my heart is set toward God Himself.
God is light, and once you turn to Him, you are in the light of
His face, and you are illuminated inside. This is a certainty.

VI. AN ILLUMINATED HEART

In Matthew 6:22-23 the Lord Jesus said, "The lamp of
the body is the eye. If therefore your eye is single, your whole
body will be illuminated. But if your eye is evil, your
whole body will be dark. If then the light that is in you is
darkness, how great the darkness!" This word shows us that
someone's heart may not be illuminated, but dark. Why the
darkness? The darkness exists because his heart is not pointing toward God. At least, it is off a little, thus losing the light
of God's face. Preceding and following this word, the Lord
said, "For where your treasure is, there will your heart be
also...No one can serve two masters...you cannot serve God
and mammon." This word tells us that the heart in man is
dark because it is not after God. Rather, it is after things
other than God. God is light, and if our heart is pointing
toward God, surely we will be illuminated inside. But whenever our heart shall turn away from God, immediately we are
dark inside. One who prays must always exercise to have an
illuminated heart.

We often hear people say, "Oh, I am so confused and dark
within, these days." This condition reveals to us that the

heart of such a person is not fully turned to God and needs to be dealt with properly. This dealing is not just with sins or the world, but even more, it deals with the direction of the heart. Does your heart purely desire God alone, or does it desire other things besides God? If you seek after some fruits of your work, the blessings of God, or spiritual enjoyments, then your heart is pointing in the wrong direction. Once the direction of the heart is wrong, immediately there is darkness within.

Brothers, seriously speaking, not many Christians today are illuminated within. This is because there are still many mixtures in their hearts. They do not seek God with a pure heart. Let us give some illustrations. Suppose you preached the gospel and only two people were saved, but when another preached, twenty people were saved. Following this you did not feel good in your heart. This would prove that you were neither pure nor single. Again, suppose you were in the process of purchasing property for building a meeting hall in your locality, and a certain church was burdened from the Lord to supply the needs of several other churches. While other churches received one hundred thousand or eighty thousand dollars, your locality only received eight thousand. Would you feel happy or not? Now, suppose we change the situation: the supplying church had only eight thousand dollars, yet she gave none to any other church but gave the whole amount to your locality. Surely you would be beaming with smiles, thanking and praising the Lord. It was the same eight thousand dollars, yet your reaction was altogether different! As another example, suppose you and another brother were roommates. A responsible brother of the church goes to visit your roommate for five minutes today, ten minutes tomorrow, and fifteen minutes the day after tomorrow. He does this for four consecutive weeks, yet he never comes to fellowship with you. How would you feel about this? Surely you would grumble inside. These reactions in your heart prove that your heart is not pure. Again, on the Lord's day at the table meeting both of us prayed. Others gave an amen after you had prayed three sentences, but they said amen to every sentence I prayed—they followed me with amens all the time. Would you be happy or not? You would not be happy because everyone said only a few amens to you, but many to me.

Brothers, these things may seem trivial, but they prove to us how much we are off, and complicated in our hearts. Do not believe that we are so good. If someone would write a biography about us, I think there would be no need to write about anything other than our heart. Because he would not be able to exhaust this one subject, that is, the movements of our heart from morning to evening and from evening to morning. With such a record, you can know how much your heart has been off and how much it refuses God. Such a condition of the heart is the reason that many people are not illuminated. The reason we are dark and not illuminated within is because we are not facing the light. Whenever we serve two masters and love things besides God, our inner eye becomes evil. This is a certainty.

Therefore, brothers, the price of obtaining light is to have the heart turned to God. If one wishes to have light and revelation, there is only one secret: seek God alone with a single and pure heart. If the needle in man is pointing toward many things—in the morning pointing toward benefits, in the afternoon toward position, another time toward men's approval, and in the prayer meeting toward men's amens—how could one, being so complicated inside, have the light? Therefore, to learn how to pray, one needs to deal with his heart so that he may be illuminated within.

VII. THE INFLUENCES ON THE HEART

Influences on our heart come from the four parts which constitute the heart. If one has a problem in his conscience, his heart is affected. If there is accusation in the conscience, surely there will be condemnation in the heart. In the same manner, if one's mind is perverted and improper, his heart becomes unreasonable. It may be plainly six, yet he would say it is eight. Such unreasonableness issues from an unregulated mind, and an unregulated mind can affect the heart. Not only so, if one loves many things other than God in his emotions, it will also affect the heart. Also, if a man's will is so stubborn that he never reconsiders once he has made a decision, this also affects the heart, making it hard. For instance, someone may be moved by the gospel he has heard, but since he has already determined that there is no place for God in his ambitious plans, he remains stubbornly unchanged. Thus, his heart becomes very hard.

Please remember, therefore, in order to have a proper heart, the conscience, the mind, the emotion, and the will need to be dealt with adequately. If there is offense in the conscience, it is inevitable that there will be condemnation in the heart. If the mind becomes irrational, the heart will surely be improper. Similarly, if the emotion has its private desires, then the heart certainly will not be able to love God. And if the will is stubborn and unchanging, the heart will surely become hard.

The influences over the heart are the influences over the soul and the spirit. Therefore, the heart represents our whole being. To have a proper heart, we need to deal thoroughly with all the parts of the soul and the spirit. On the other hand, if our heart is right, then our whole being is right. If there is no condemnation in the heart, there is no accusation in the conscience. Once the heart is set right, the mind is spontaneously regulated. If the heart absolutely loves God, then the emotion is surely proper. At the same time, if the heart is soft and not one bit hard, then there is no problem with the will. Hence, a man can only be right when his heart is right.

VIII. THE HEART AND PRAYER

When a man's heart is true, pure, without condemnation, and illuminated, being normal in every aspect, he is able to pray. The heart and prayer are absolutely related. Although the spirit is the organ for prayer, one still cannot pray unless his heart has been dealt with properly. And even if he could pray, he would not be able to believe that God would answer. As long as there is a problem with the heart, it is not possible to pray.

As there is such an intimate relationship between the heart and prayer, it can almost be said that if you would just deal with your heart, that, in itself, is almost as good as prayer. Then all you need to do is to cry out to God a little. Many times our prayers do not have much weight or value. The main reason is because our hearts are not proper. First John 3:19 through 22 tells us that if our heart condemns us not, we have boldness toward God, and whatsoever we ask, we receive of Him. Therefore, it is necessary to deal with the heart in order that our prayers may have weight and standing.

IX. THE HEART FOR PRAYER

The heart for prayer is a heart that is truthful and pure, not bent, false, or doubting. It seeks God alone and nothing else. It is also without condemnation or offense. It is also a heart turned to God, aiming only at Him. It is further an illuminated heart which is full of light and is in the light of God's face. Finally, it is a heart that is under the proper influence of the various parts. One who prays needs such a heart for prayer.

Chapter Eleven

PRAYER AND ABIDING IN THE LORD

John 15:7 says, "If you abide in Me and My words abide in you, ask whatever you will, and it shall come to pass to you." This Bible verse may be divided into four points. The first point is, "you abide in Me." The second is, "and My words abide in you." Verses 4 and 5 speak of our abiding in the Lord and He in us. But in verse 7, "I" is changed to "My words"—"You abide in Me and My words abide in you." "I" being changed to "My words," means that I have something to explain to you. This may be clarified by the following example: if I were to go to your home, first my person would go there; then, after I had been there for a short while, I would speak and reveal the intention of my visit. Hence, when it says here, "My words abide in you," this is a step forward. Third it says, "whatever you will." Because of the Lord's speaking in us, we begin to desire something, and this desire is something issuing out of the Lord's words. Fourth it says, "ask, and it shall come to pass to you." When we thus abide in the Lord, His words abide in us, and there is the desiring in us that comes out of His words; finally, "will" becomes "ask." This asking is not an ordinary prayer. It is a specific prayer. Whenever asking is mentioned in the Bible, it invariably refers to a specific prayer. Hence, this asking will be answered by God.

This verse of the Bible mentions two things: on one hand, it says that we abide in the Lord, and on the other hand, it says the Lord's words abide in us. Consequently, the matter of prayer issues forth from the Lord's words. All prevailing prayers, prayers that can be counted effective before the Lord, must surely be the result of our abiding in the Lord and allowing His words to abide in us.

First John 1:5-7 says, "This then is the message which we have heard of him, and declare unto you, that God is light, and in him is no darkness at all. If we say that we have fellowship with him, and walk in darkness, we lie, and do not the truth: But if we walk in the light, as he is in the light, we have fellowship one with another, and the blood of Jesus Christ his Son cleanseth us from all sin."

These few verses cover three things: fellowship, the light, and the blood. If we have fellowship with God, surely we will be in the light, for God is light. When there is fellowship, then there is light. When light comes there is the need for the blood.

First John 2:27-28 says, "But the anointing which ye have received of him abideth in you, and ye need not that any man teach you: but as the same anointing teacheth you of all things, and is truth, and is no lie, and even as it hath taught you, ye shall abide in him. And now, little children, abide in him; that, when he shall appear, we may have confidence, and not be ashamed before him at his coming."

These two verses of the Bible also point out three things: one, "the anointing"; two, "as the anointing teacheth you, ye abide in the Lord"; and three, "abide in the Lord." The abiding in the Lord here is the same as that which is spoken of in John 15. The anointing is one thing, and abiding in the Lord according to the anointing is another thing. Finally, it re-emphasizes this abiding by saying, "My little children, abide in the Lord."

In the past ten chapters we have spoken mostly concerning the meaning of prayer and the organs used in prayer, or, the course of prayer. Now we will begin to touch something regarding prayer itself by finding out what is the nature of man's real prayer before God.

Whatever task a person performs, he must be the kind of person constituted for that task. One who serves as a physician must be a person who is a qualified physician. One who serves as a teacher must be a person who *is* a teacher. One who serves as a mother must be a person who *is* a mother.

Likewise, you also need to be a praying one so that you can function in prayer. Generally speaking, a man of prayer is one who abides in the Lord. Now we shall see what abiding in the Lord means.

I. THE MEANING OF ABIDING IN THE LORD

A. In the Lord

The experience of abiding in the Lord is based on the fact of being in the Lord. If you are not in the Lord, there is no way for you to abide in the Lord. This fact of our being in the Lord was accomplished long ago. The accomplishment may be divided into two stages. When the Lord finished redemption on the cross, He joined us to Himself, putting us into Him. This is the first stage. Then when we were regenerated, the Holy Spirit came into us and *practically* joined us to Christ, putting us into Him. This is the second stage.

Romans 6:3 says that we were baptized into Christ Jesus. By this we can see that to be baptized is to be put into Christ. The phrase "believe in the Lord," according to the original Greek text, should be properly rendered as "believe *into* the Lord." The "into" in "believe into the Lord" and the "into" in "baptized into Christ" are the same word. Romans 6 says "baptized into," and John 3:16 says "believe into." One is to be baptized into, and the other is to believe into. In baptism you are baptized *into* Christ, and in believing you believe *into* Christ. When we believe in the Lord, the Spirit puts us completely *into* Christ and causes us to have an organic union with Christ. Thereafter, in practicality, we become those who are in Christ. Hence, 2 Corinthians 5:17 says that if any man is in Christ, he is a new creation. Everyone who desires to abide in Christ needs to see the fact of being in Christ. If someone does not see this fact it is useless to exhort him to abide in Christ. It will even be a hardship on him, for no matter how hard he tries to abide in Christ, he can never make it. But if he has the light and revelation that he is in Christ, he will see that to abide is an easy matter. He will realize that it is not necessary to seek abiding, because he is already in. This has already been accomplished by Christ.

Let us give a little illustration. Suppose you are a member of the Jones family. Since your birth you have been in the Jones family. As you were born into the Jones family, quite naturally you live with them. But suppose according to your knowledge, you are an outsider, yet you insist on living in the Jones's house. That is not easy. First you must see that you are one who is in the Jones family. This is an accomplished fact based on your birth. You are, therefore, one of the Jones family, and all you need to do is to acknowledge this fact. Now what is required of you is that you remain there by living at home. In the same principle, if you desire to abide in the Lord, you must realize a fact. Something has happened to you and you are now already in Christ. Before you were saved you were born in Adam. But after you were saved, God moved you out of the realm of Adam into the realm of Christ. The fact of being in Christ is now accomplished. "In" is a marvelous word.

B. Abide in the Lord

The word "abide" means to remain. Abide in the Lord may also be translated as remain in the Lord. Ephesians 3:17 says that Christ dwells in our hearts through faith. The word "dwells" means to make your home. When you live in a house, that means you dwell there. When you go to a certain place and stay there for ten days, that means you remain there. The word "abide" in the phrase "abide in the Lord" does not mean to dwell or to reside, but it means to remain, to stay. As you are a saved one and you are already in the Lord, what is required of you now is that you do not leave, but remain in Him.

To illustrate, suppose you were baptized yesterday, and you clearly sensed that you had been joined to the Lord and that you are in Him. Last night, however, a friend came and insisted on taking you to a movie. While you were about to go with him, you sensed there was something wrong between you and the Lord. As you were considering what might be wrong, your friend continued to persuade you, and you decided to go with him. At that moment you felt that your fellowship with the Lord had been cut off. You felt that way because you did not remain in the Lord. You may be a saved one and thus in the Lord, but experientially you may not always remain in Him. In your experience it seems at times that you have walked out of the Lord, and your fellowship with the Lord has been broken.

Again, for example, you have just been saved and now you have a clear sense that you are joined to the Lord. But today it so happened that something greatly provoked you. While you were about to lose your temper, you felt something was wrong inside. Nevertheless, you went ahead and lost your temper. And because you lost your temper, you knew within yourself that the fellowship with the Lord had been interrupted. It seemed as if you had walked out of the Lord. This means you did not remain in Him.

To remain in the Lord is to abide in the Lord. When you thus remain in the Lord, you have continuous fellowship with Him. To be in the Lord is a matter of union. To abide in the Lord is a matter of fellowship. Fellowship is made possible by our being put into an organic union with the Lord. To have unceasing fellowship is to abide, and to abide is to maintain this unceasing fellowship.

The theme of the first Epistle of John is fellowship. In the first chapter of that book it tells us that we who have Christ as life do have fellowship with God. The life which we have received in us causes us to have fellowship with Him. The Gospel of John speaks of life, and the first Epistle of John speaks of fellowship. The Gospel of John continuously shows us how the Lord came and entered into men to be their life and to save them. First John continues to speak of the fellowship. As you have been saved and have Christ as life, this life will cause you to have fellowship with God. First John 1 speaks of fellowship, and chapter two speaks of abiding in the Lord. The abiding in the Lord which is spoken of in chapter two is the fellowship spoken of in chapter one. What does it mean to abide in the Lord? It means to have an uninterrupted fellowship with the Lord, not to come out of the fellowship, and to extend the union with the Lord.

II. MAINTAINING THE ABIDING IN THE LORD

Abiding in the Lord is the way to maintain and continue in our experience of the fact of being in the Lord. As soon as we are saved God puts us into Christ. But how can we continually maintain the fellowship with the Lord? First John points out two means: the blood and the anointing.

A. The Cleansing of the Blood

First John 1 directly and clearly shows us that we need to maintain the fellowship through the blood. God is light. Once you have fellowship with God and touch Him, you cannot escape being in the light. Fellowship places you before God, and it also puts you in the light. Once you are in the light, you will inevitably see your sins. For example, at first glance the air surrounding us seems to be very clean. If, however, we observe that same air under intense sunlight, immediately we will notice that there are innumerable dirt particles floating in that air. Without the exposing of the light of the sun we would not be able to see them. Likewise, if we lack the fellowship with God and are therefore not in the light, we can never be conscious of our own mistakes. But once we enter into fellowship with God and we are put in the light, we discover that we are full of impurities. There are impurities in our mind, our emotion, our will, our intention, our motive, and even in the consciousness of our spirit. Once we are in the light, our condition surely becomes manifest. And once it becomes manifest, our conscience will condemn us. If there is not the cleansing of the blood, offenses will definitely be present in our conscience. Once there are offenses in our conscience, the fellowship between God and us is interrupted, and we thus come out from the presence of the Lord.

Furthermore, in our daily living there are still many actual sins which could offend our conscience. We have previously mentioned such things as going to the movies and losing our temper. Without any need of teaching from others, you, yourself know too well that these things are wrong. As one who is saved, who is in Christ, and who is in the light, you automatically have this feeling. Nevertheless, because of your weakness, you may have done such things. And because you did those things, there were offenses in your conscience, and you felt that you had come out of the presence of the Lord.

At that very moment you need to be cleansed by the blood of our Lord Jesus. If we are in the light, as God is in the light, then we have fellowship one with another (1 John 1:7). Under the light of such a fellowship, we see our sins and spontaneously confess them before the Lord. The blood of Jesus His Son will then cleanse us and remove the offenses from our conscience (1 John 1:9). Then we sense that we are again in fellowship with the Lord. The blood is able to restore and recover our fellowship. This recovery is the maintenance.

In the Old Testament, on the day of atonement, the high priest would bring the blood into the Holy Place and put it upon the incense altar. Then he would bring it into the Holy of Holies and sprinkle it upon the mercy seat, which is to sprinkle it before God. Hebrews 9 tells us that the Lord Jesus also brought with Him the blood which He shed on the cross, into the presence of God and sprinkled it before God. To this day, the blood of the Lord Jesus is still speaking well of us before God. It speaks on our behalf and is the ground of atonement. It is based on this blood that we confess our offenses before God. When we thus confess, the Spirit applies the effectiveness of the cleansing of the blood upon our conscience. Our conscience is purged of all its offenses, so that there is no more barrier between God and us, and the fellowship is restored. Hence, our abiding in the Lord is first maintained by means of the blood.

B. The Anointing of the Ointment

The anointing of the ointment is the anointing spoken of in 1 John chapter two. In the New Testament age, God comes to man as the Holy Spirit. The Holy Spirit is not just the oil, but the ointment. God comes to man to be the ointment moving within him. This moving is the anointing. First John 2:27 speaks not only of the Spirit being the ointment in us, but even more of the ointment anointing in us. Hence, the anointing of the ointment does not speak of the ointment itself. Rather, it speaks of the anointing action of the ointment, which is the moving of the Holy Spirit in us. The continuous moving of the Spirit in us keeps us remaining in the fellowship of God and thus abiding in the Lord. Thus, the anointing also maintains the fact of our being in the Lord.

Therefore, the first means by which fellowship is maintained is the cleansing of the blood, and the second is the anointing of the ointment. This precisely corresponds to the types in the Old Testament. The types in the Old Testament show that when man desired to contact God and fellowship with God, he had to first sprinkle the blood and then apply the ointment. When speaking of maintaining the fellowship, the New Testament brings up the matters of sprinkling the blood and applying the ointment. The sprinkling of the blood is to cleanse away all that should not be there. The anointing of the ointment is to anoint us with the elements of God, even with God Himself. It is just like someone painting furniture. As a result of the painting action, the paint is applied to the furniture. The Spirit coming to man is God coming to man. And by the Spirit moving and anointing in man, God is wrought into man.

Therefore, on the negative side, the blood cleanses away all the things that we should not have. On the positive side, the ointment anoints us with what we should have. What we should not have are the sins, and what we should have is God Himself. By the continual cleansing and anointing of the blood and the ointment, we maintain our union with the Lord always.

The Lamb and the Dove in John 1 are parallel to the blood and the ointment. The blood is the Lamb, and the ointment is the Dove. The Lamb denotes the Lord shedding His blood for us on the cross to take away our sins. The Dove denotes the Spirit coming to man to add the elements of God into man. Hence, we must learn to constantly receive the blood for the cleansing of our sins and to move according to the anointing of the ointment within. On one hand, as soon as we sense we are wrong, we should immediately confess our mistake and receive the cleansing of the blood. On the other hand, whenever the Spirit moves within us, we should immediately move according to the consciousness of that anointing. Thus, we abide and remain in the Lord. This should be our continuous and uninterrupted practice.

III. A LIFE OF ABIDING IN THE LORD

The Christian life is a life of abiding in the Lord. If you continuously abide in the Lord, your life will surely be holy, victorious, and spiritual. Every aspect of our Christian life is included in the life of abiding in the Lord. There are several points in this living that we need to learn properly:

A. Walking according to the Spirit

To walk according to the Spirit is to walk according to the anointing of the ointment. We have said that God comes to us as the ointment within us, always anointing us and giving us consciousness. If we walk according to this consciousness, we are walking according to the Spirit. For example, while you are speaking, if your inner consciousness prohibits you from going on, you ought to stop. If your inner consciousness urges you to take some action, you should obey it and take that particular action. You may be about to express a certain attitude. If it seems that there is an inner feeling restraining you, then you should stop quickly and not express it. Whether in great things or small things, learn to follow the inner consciousness. To obey the inner consciousness is to walk according to the Spirit. And to walk according to the Spirit is to obey the anointing of the ointment. This is to abide in the Lord according to the anointing of the ointment.

Immediately following our salvation, we have the Spirit as the ointment anointing us and moving in us. Hence, we inevitably have a consciousness of the anointing. Our responsibility is to strictly take heed to that consciousness in the depths of our being. Do not think or reason with your mind. Once you think, consider, argue, or analyze, you will surely come out of your spirit and no longer remain in the abiding. Your thoughts, your reasoning, and your natural insight can often interrupt your fellowship with the Lord. Therefore, pay no attention to them, but take care of the consciousness in the depths of your being. The more you walk according to this consciousness, you will discover that you are more deeply abiding in the Lord. And, simultaneously and spontaneously, your life will be one of abiding in the Lord.

B. Dealing with Sins

Within we have the inherent sinful nature, and without we live in a society which is full of sinful defilements. Unconsciously, we are being contaminated by sin daily. Therefore, if we truly walk according to the Spirit and live continually in the Lord, we will surely have the consciousness of sin. Then we should confess our sins before the Lord, and by His leading depart from them. Due to the sinful environment without and the sinful nature within us, it is a very difficult matter to live daily without being defiled by sin. Very often, unconsciously, sin will come to trouble our mind, damage our emotion, defile our spirit, and cause us to be sinful in our actions. Hence, it is only by the blood, as we confess our sins again and again, that we are able to abide in the Lord continuously.

It is very seldom that one who truly knows how to pray can do so without first confessing his sins. The more one walks according to the Spirit, the more he will discover that he has numerous sins within and without. The more he walks according to the Spirit, the more sensitive he will be toward the consciousness of sin. If he commits a slight mistake, he will sense it immediately and will deal with it. The more dealings he has, the more illuminated he is within and the more sensitive he becomes. The more dealings he has, the more he becomes transparent, at ease, fresh inside, and ultimately, the more he lives in the Lord. This is a life of abiding in the Lord.

C. Absolutely Having No Barrier between You and the Lord

Morally speaking, some things may not be considered sinful, but if doing one of those things causes a barrier to exist between you and the Lord, that thing needs to be dealt with. The life of abiding in the Lord not only disallows sins, it also disallows barriers. For example, you may have a short talk with a brother. The words may be proper, and the thing that you talk about may not be sinful. But if after the conversation there is a barrier between you and the Lord, then that is still a sin. Because you spoke something contrary to the inner consciousness, it was a sin of disobedience. God told Saul, "To obey is better than sacrifice, and to hearken than the fat of rams. For rebellion is as the sin of witchcraft, and stubbornness is as iniquity and idolatry" (1 Sam. 15:22-23). When one disobeys God, this disobedience becomes a sin which creates a barrier between him and the Lord.

Hence, a life of abiding in the Lord requires us not only to walk continuously according to the Spirit, deal with sins, and depart from sins, but also to always have no barrier between us and the Lord. Regardless how good a certain matter is, if by doing it a barrier is created between me and the Lord, then I should not do it. Do not go by the moral standard, but take the Lord Himself as the standard. Sometimes you may give some money to others or help someone. These things are really good in themselves, but sometimes the Lord forbids us to do them. If you would do them in spite of His prohibition, even the giving of money or helping someone will interrupt your fellowship with the Lord and create a barrier. Refrain from doing anything that would cause you to be separated from the Lord. In order to maintain a life of abiding in the Lord, not only sins need to be dealt with, but any barriers also need to be removed.

IV. THE RESULTS OF ABIDING IN THE LORD

A. Understanding God's Desire

Once man abides in the Lord, spontaneously he touches God's feeling and understands God's desire. In the Old Testament, Abraham was an example of this. Because he continually remained before God, God could not refrain from telling Abraham of His intention. Psalm 32:8 says that God guides us with His eyes. This is like the Chinese saying that one acts by the wink or hint given with the eyes. If you live in the fellowship, you will understand what the Bible means when it says God guides us with His eyes. We need not be as the horse or as the mule, which have no understanding, so that God has to bridle us with headstall, bit, and reins, in order that we may understand His desire. We only need to live in the fellowship, remain in His presence, and draw near to Him. Then spontaneously we will be able to understand His temperament, His disposition, and the principles of His doings. It is as if in our spirit we catch a glimpse of the Lord's eyes and thus spontaneously touch His feeling and understand His desire.

B. Having God's Desire

After we have touched God's feeling and understood His intention, spontaneously we will have His desire in us. At that moment, His desire becomes our desire, and what He wants is exactly what we want.

V. PRAYER THAT RESULTS FROM ABIDING IN THE LORD

After we have touched God's feeling, understood His intention, and are also able to desire what He desires, then we pray. This is the very thing that is spoken of in John 15:7. "If you abide in Me and My words abide in you, ask whatever you will, and it shall come to pass to you." This wish does not come out of the one who prays. Rather, it comes out from that which God has anointed into him. Since this desire is God's desire, when he prays, God answers.

Some, shortly after they have been saved, read this verse in John 15 and then they say, "This promise of the Lord is truly wonderful. I can ask whatever I will and He will bring it to pass to me." So they begin to ask according to whatever they want. Eventually, they find that what they ask for is not granted. This is not because the Lord's promise fails to materialize. It is because they take the Lord's promise out of context. They pray without first fulfilling the necessary requirements. They misunderstand the meaning of the verse. John 15:7 covers a total of four points. First, "you abide in Me." Second, "My words abide in you." Third, since My words speak forth My intention, it becomes the desire in you so that whatever you desire is what I desire. Fourth, as a result, such prayer will surely be answered by God. Now we understand that the desire in our prayer does not originate from man, but it is what God desires. First, man continuously abides in the Lord. Then God becomes the words in man so that man is able to understand God's intention. This produces in man a desire which is God's desire. When man prays according to this desire, God has no choice but to answer it. This then is to "ask and you shall receive." This prayer is a prayer resulting from abiding in the Lord.

CHAPTER TWELVE

PRAYER AND THE LORD'S WORD

John 15:7 says, "If you abide in Me and My words abide in you...."

Colossians 3:16-17 says, "Let the word of Christ dwell in you richly, in all wisdom teaching and admonishing one another in psalms, hymns, and spiritual songs, singing with grace in your hearts to God; And in everything, whatever you do in word or in work, do all in the name of the Lord Jesus, giving thanks to God the Father through Him."

This Scripture first tells us to let the word of the Lord dwell in us. Then it says we need to have singing, thanksgiving, and praising, which are all related to the matter of prayer. When there is the indwelling of the Word, there is prayer.

Ephesians 5:18b through 20 says, "But be filled in spirit, speaking to one another in psalms and hymns and spiritual songs, singing and psalming with your heart to the Lord, giving thanks at all times for all things in the name of our Lord Jesus Christ to God and the Father."

This portion of the Scripture first tells us that we should be filled in spirit. It goes on to say that we need to have prayer by singing, praising, and giving thanks. We all know that these two books, Ephesians and Colossians, run parallel to one another. They contain many similar points which are expressed in slightly different words. For example, the passages quoted here say that Christians should always sing, praise, and give thanks to God. Colossians tells us that this is the issue of the Lord's word indwelling us. Ephesians says that this is the result of our being filled in spirit. Although these verses express it in different ways, in reality they refer to the same thing from the same source, which is the Lord Himself. Because the Lord fills you within, singing, giving thanks, and praising come forth from you. This Lord Who is in you, is both the Spirit and the Word. When you are filled with His words, you are filled in spirit. When you are filled in spirit, you are filled with His words. Hence, His words in us are spirit.

Now we shall look at the relationship between prayer and the Lord's word.

I. THE LORD'S MOVING

Prayer is a moving of the Lord in man. True prayers are God speaking forth His words from within man and through man. In the matter of prayer, nothing is more crucial than the understanding of this point. From the beginning we have pointed out clearly that prayer does not mean that man has a need and thus asks God to fulfill it. This is the human concept. The prayer which the Bible speaks of is that God has a need, and He enters into man, causing him to be conscious of that need. Then He operates within man, moves man, and places a burden on man to pray forth that particular need. This is prayer. We need to start from here if we wish to see the relationship between prayer and the Lord's word. Because God moves in us, we can pray. Prayers that come out of ourselves are of no spiritual value. What God wants are prayers that issue from His moving within us—prayers which are initiated by Him.

II. GOD'S COMING

In order to move in us God must come to us. If there is still a distance between Him and us, He will not be able to move in us. But when He comes to us to motivate us, He does not take the position of God, nor of the Lord, but of the Spirit. Whenever God comes to us, He is the Spirit.

Due to a lack of understanding of the mysterious things of God, men are often confused, and therefore debate a great deal concerning the trinity of the Godhead. We can understand the mystery of God's coming to man, in a very simple way. Whenever the New Testament speaks of God coming to man, entering into man, descending upon man, or operating, moving, and stirring within man, it always speaks of the Spirit. If God does not have any dealings with man, He is simply afar off and outside man. But as the Spirit, He comes to enter into man and have dealings with man.

In the New Testament, the first mention that God is Spirit is in the Gospel of John, chapter four. There the Lord Jesus says, "God is Spirit; and those who worship Him must worship in spirit..." The emphasis of this verse is His contact with man. God coming to man and entering into man is Spirit.

III. GOD'S EXPLANATION

The Holy Spirit coming to man and entering into man is not just for the infilling and the outpouring. It is also for Him to become the indwelling words of God. If God's coming to man is merely His coming, with no words, there would be no way for man to understand His intention. There is no way His intention can be explained without words. Suppose someone comes into my home, but he does not say a word. That would be quite difficult for me. John 14:17 says that when the Spirit comes, He enters into us; 15:4 says that we abide in the Lord, and the Lord also abides in us. Then, verse seven says, "If you abide in Me, and My words abide in you..." Here the Lord becomes the words and explanation in us.

Likewise, in Colossians it says that our giving thanks and our praises are due to the word of the Lord. In Ephesians it says that we thank and praise due to the Spirit. If there is only the filling of the Spirit but there is no word, how can you have psalms and hymns? You cannot, for there is only the stirring but not the explanation. For example, this morning I may feel the need to pray, but there is no word or explanation in me telling me what to pray for or how to pray. The best I could do would be to weep or to shout a few hallelujahs. I could not pray thoroughly.

Hence, the Spirit that comes to us must become the explanation in us. Once it becomes the explanation, it is the word. The Gospel of John tells us clearly that the words which the Lord speaks to us are spirit. When the Spirit in us causes us to understand, then it is the word. Sometimes we may have inspiration inside, but we cannot understand because the Spirit has not yet become words and there is a lack of explanation. Then, one day He explains it to us, that is, the Spirit becomes the word. Then, and only then, can we understand His intention.

One who ministers the Word usually has this experience: when he is about to stand up to speak a word, he feels he has the inspiration and the burden within him. However, he still does not know specifically what he should speak. Then, as he stands and speaks, he has an inner sense, and the more he speaks the clearer he becomes. The Spirit within has become the word. The same is true with prayer. For example, someone waking in the morning may feel the burden to pray, but he does not know for what he should pray. He thus goes before God, and as he prays, he tries to sense his inner feeling. As a result, the inner consciousness becomes the word, and the word is then expressed. One sentence comes forth, and the next one follows immediately. After the prayer is finished, the inner burden has been discharged. This means the Spirit has become the word.

Real prayers, therefore, are the outcome of God's moving within us. This moving is carried out through the Spirit, and the Spirit needs to become the word, the explanation. Thus, we are able to express our prayers.

IV. GOD'S EXPRESSION

Explanation is an inward understanding, whereas expression is an outward declaration. Every true prayer is just like a weighty message, all the words of prayer being the expression of the Spirit. It can almost be said that the words of prayer are the very Spirit. No wonder the Lord Jesus said His words are spirit. For whatever He speaks, it is the expression of the Spirit. In principle, our prayers should be the same.

In prayer we have often really touched the spirit, enjoyed the Lord's presence very much, and had the anointing of the ointment. At other times we would have to admit that our prayer was not so good. The more we prayed, the more dry and dead we were inside. The more we prayed, the fewer words we had. Where does the difference between these two conditions lie? The basic issue is: while we were praying, did the Spirit come to us and explain God's intention to us? If we have such an explanation, then we can express it accordingly. Thus, the more we pray, the more we are inspired. The more we pray, the more we have the anointing. The more we pray, the more we touch the spirit, and the fresher and livelier we are. For in that prayer the Spirit comes forth with the words that we express. On the contrary, at other times there may be no moving of the Spirit while we pray, and thus our words are not the expression of the Spirit. Then it is simply we ourselves speaking, and such a prayer will spontaneously be dried up.

Real prayers are the result of God's moving in us. God's moving starts with the Spirit first coming to us and then going a step further to become the explanation. The explanation is the word. Once the words are present in our consciousness, they must be expressed. When we speak forth those words, that is prayer.

V. THE RELATIONSHIP BETWEEN THE WORD AND THE SPIRIT

The Lord's word to us comes in two stages. One stage is the words in the Scripture, and the other stage is the words in the Spirit. Colossians says that we should let the word of Christ dwell in us richly. We must believe that this refers to the words in the Scripture. We often encourage the brothers and sisters to saturate themselves with the Scriptures. The reason for this is that we might remember the words of the Lord and thus retain them within us. Then, at a certain time, when the Spirit comes to us, He will express Himself with the Scripture words that we have remembered and retained within us. At this time, these words will become the words of the Spirit.

When we speak of the relationship between prayer and the Lord's word, it includes these two aspects: the words of the Spirit and the words of the Scripture; or the Lord's word in the Scripture and the Lord's word in the Spirit. In reality, these two words are just one. However, if the words in the

Scripture do not become the words in the Spirit, then they are words merely in our memory and in our intellect but have not entered into our spirit. It is only when the Spirit comes to mingle with these words that these words become the words in our spirit. This is the relationship between the Word and the Spirit.

VI. RECEIVING THE LORD'S WORD

There are two steps in receiving the Lord's word. The first is to receive the word of the Bible, and the second is to receive that word explained by the Spirit. Or we may say that first we receive the Lord's word from the Bible into us, and then we receive the Lord's word from the Spirit. Without the first step it is very difficult to have the second. Whoever is very poor in receiving the word from the Bible cannot be rich in receiving the word from the Spirit. To obtain the word richly from the Spirit, one needs to receive the word of the Bible richly into himself. Hence, we declare that we need to read the Bible, understand the Bible, and remember its words. This is to allow the words of the Bible to be stored in us richly.

Dear brothers and sisters, not only prayer, but the ministry of the Word also requires this deposit. If one who ministers the Word does not regularly store the words of the Bible within him, his ministry will not be powerful. When others minister on the same topic, the more they minister, the richer they are, and the more words flow out. When you minister, you cannot speak much, because you quickly exhaust your words. What is the reason? It is because you do not have a sufficient deposit inside. Therefore, everyone who ministers must be diligent to read the Bible.

A leading brother once conversed with me about the matter of ministering the Word. He said that there are two prerequisites to a proper ministry. First, there should be the rich, regular, storing of the Word. Second, when the time comes, there should also be the ability to receive instant utterance, burden, and inspiration. After he had told us these two principles he said, "Look at Brother A. When he speaks, you can tell that, although he has the inspiration, there is not enough storage in him to match the inspiration. Then look at Brother B. He really has an adequate supply within him, but he is not able to receive the instant inspiration. As a result, his ministering is very stiff." That conversation left me with a very deep impression. Truly, a proper, powerful, and living ministry must possess both of these two requirements: sufficient storage, and the ability to receive instant inspiration.

These two steps apply not only to the ministering of the Word, but also to prayer. We really feel sorry for some brothers who always pray the same old words because they neither have the reserve nor the inspiration. What is the reserve? The reserve is the Lord's word in the Bible having been stored in our being. What is inspiration? Inspiration is the Lord's word received from the Spirit. Day by day, read the Bible thoroughly, proficiently, and properly. Receive and store it within you. Then when the time comes for you to minister or pray, as the Spirit moves in you, the inspiration will come and mingle with the reserve within you. Once you receive such inspiration, it is hard to say whether it is the word of the Bible or the word of the Spirit. You can say that the word of the Bible is the word of the Spirit and vice versa. At this point, the Word has become spirit. We must, therefore, learn to receive the Lord's word. Otherwise, we will not know how to minister or how to pray. If we want our ministering to be weighty and our prayers valuable and suitable to God's heart, then it is absolutely essential that we learn to receive the Lord's word.

I repeat, there are two steps in the receiving of the Lord's word. One step is to read the Bible and receive the Lord's word therein. The other is to be inspired and receive the Lord's word in the spirit. The former requires the long-term effort of reading the Bible daily, thoroughly, and getting it into you. The latter requires you to be able to receive inspiration at any time. Thus, whenever inspiration comes, you will be able to express it with the words of the Bible which you have received. If you have this ability, then you are able to minister and to pray. First, take in the words of the Bible, then, when inspiration comes, the words will become the words in the spirit. At that time, what you pray forth is prayer, and what you speak forth is ministry.

Read the Scripture well and you will be able to pray well. But this does not mean that simply by being well-versed in the Scriptures you will be able to pray very well. Some really know the Bible by heart. In their prayer, they can quote from Genesis to Revelation. But while listening to their praying, you realize that it is issuing altogether from their dead mind with dead letters, and is not in life at all. This is not what we mean by receiving the word of the Lord. What we mean is that you must daily receive the word of the Bible into you through the Spirit. Then at a certain time, when you receive inspiration, the Holy Spirit will make the words which you received of the Bible, His words. He will interpret and speak them once more into your spirit. Then these words will become spirit, the living word, and the word of life. This is what we mean by receiving the Lord's word.

VII. THE WORDS BECOMING SPIRIT

We have previously fellowshipped the matter of the spirit becoming the word. Now let us examine the matter of the Word becoming spirit. Words becoming spirit means that the words of the Bible which you have read, or the words of expounding the Bible which you have heard, have become spirit in you. The words which you have received will, at a certain time, become spirit in you. Brothers, please recall your experiences of prayer and you will realize that a good, spiritual prayer is the issue of the Spirit of God mingling with you. You are not reciting the Bible, but rather praying the words with which the Spirit has touched and moved you. What you pray is a mingling of the words of the Bible and of the Spirit. At this point, the words which you have formerly received and stored in you will become the words in the Spirit. This means the words in you have become spirit.

CHAPTER THIRTEEN

THE CROSS AND PRAYER

Leviticus 16:18-19 says, "And he shall go out unto the altar that is before the LORD, and make an atonement for it; and shall take of the blood of the bullock, and of the blood of the goat, and put it upon the horns of the altar round about. And he shall sprinkle of the blood upon it with his finger seven times, and cleanse it, and hallow it from the uncleanness of the children of Israel."

In Leviticus 16:12-13 it says, "And he shall take a censer full of burning coals of fire from off the altar before the LORD, and his hands full of sweet incense beaten small, and bring it within the veil: And he shall put the incense upon the fire before the LORD, that the cloud of the incense may cover the mercy seat that is upon the testimony, that he die not."

The above two passages indicate that the priest first needed to make atonement for the people of God at the altar with the blood of the sin offering. Second, when the priest went into the Holy of Holies to burn the incense, the coals of fire which he used were to be taken from off the altar.

Exodus 30:9-10 says, "Ye shall offer no strange incense thereon, nor burnt sacrifice, nor meat offering; neither shall ye pour drink offering thereon. And Aaron shall make an atonement upon the horns of it once in a year with the blood of the sin offering of atonements; once in the year shall he make atonement upon it throughout your generations: it is most holy unto the LORD."

The above passage refers to the incense altar, not the offering altar. The tabernacle had two altars; outside was the offering altar, and inside was the incense altar. The offering altar was brass and the incense altar was gold. Both altars were places where atonements were made, and both used the same sacrifice. The tenth day of the seventh month was the day of atonement for the children of Israel. On that day the high priest took of the blood of the sin offering and sprinkled it upon the four horns of the altar outside. He also brought that blood with him into the Holy Place and sprinkled it upon the four horns of the incense altar, thus making atonement on both altars.

In Revelation 8:3 and 5 it says, "And another Angel came and stood at the altar, having a golden censer, and much incense was given to Him that He should add it to the prayers of all the saints upon the golden altar which was before the throne. And the Angel took the censer and filled it with the fire of the altar and cast it to the earth; and there were thunders and voices and lightnings and an earthquake."

"Another Angel" here refers to the Lord Jesus. By the following verse, verse 6, we know that the seven trumpets began to trumpet as a result of the Angel casting down the fire of the altar. In other words, the seven trumpets are the answer to those prayers. We need to notice that here it mentions the censer, the incense, and the prayers.

Revelation 5:8 says, "And when He took the scroll, the four living creatures and the twenty-four elders fell before the Lamb, each having a harp and golden bowls full of incense, which are the prayers of the saints."

The four living creatures and the twenty-four elders each held a harp and golden bowls. The harp is for praising, whereas the golden bowls full of incense are for prayers. In this verse, "which" refers to the bowls, not to the incense. This means the golden bowls are the prayers of the saints. This interpretation is based on the fact that in chapter eight the incense and the prayers of the saints are mentioned as two different items. The incense is Christ added to the saints' prayers. Therefore, the golden bowls here refer to the prayers of the saints.

Both Exodus and Leviticus show us that no one can enter into the tabernacle to burn incense before God and draw near to God except by passing through the altar. The altar is the cross. This means that without passing through the cross, no one can be before God and have prayer which is as fragrant incense that is acceptable to God. Hence, we still need to look at the relationship between the cross and prayer.

I. THE TWO ASPECTS OF THE CROSS

Although there are numerous aspects of the cross, with relation to prayer there are mainly two aspects. One aspect is signified by the blood that is shed on the altar, and the other is signified by the fire burnt on the altar. When anyone offers a sacrifice at the altar, after it has been accepted by God and consumed by fire there are only two things in front of him. These two things are the blood round about the altar and the coals upon the altar. As the ashes and the coals of fire are mixed together, eventually, what the offerer sees is just the blood and the fire.

The blood and the fire are the two important aspects of the cross in relation to prayer. The ability of a priest to enter the Holy Place to burn incense and pray before God is based on two things. First, that he has brought with him the blood from the offering altar outside and put it on the incense altar. Second, that he has brought with him the fire which has consumed the sacrifice offered on the offering altar outside and has put it on the incense altar to burn the incense. The blood on the incense altar inside and the blood on the offering altar outside are one and the same. The coals of fire on the incense altar inside and the coals of fire on the offering altar outside are also one and the same. In other words, the blood on the incense altar inside is based on the blood on the offering altar outside. The fire on the incense altar inside is based on the fire on the offering altar outside. The blood is for redemption of sins; the fire is for termination. Anything that is put into the fire will be terminated. The most serious damage done to anything is caused by fire. Whenever something passes through fire it is consumed. On the cross the Lord shed His blood for redemption. Through His death He also brought in a great termination. These are the two most important aspects the Lord accomplished on the cross. Every sacrifice that is placed on the offering altar not only sheds blood, but also

becomes ashes. The cross results in both redemption and termination. These are the two aspects of the cross.

In the Lord's redemption, the cross, on the one hand,
redeems us, and on the other hand, terminates us. Everyone
who prays to God must be one who has been redeemed of the
Lord in these two aspects. If one has not been sprinkled by
the blood, before God he is just like Cain, who could neither
be accepted by God nor pray. Everyone who is acceptable to
God and able to pray needs to be sprinkled with the blood.
But please remember, one who can go before God to pray not
only needs the redemption of the blood; he also needs to be
one who has been consumed at the cross. Nadab and Abihu
fell dead before God due to a problem concerning the fire,
not concerning the blood. Not having been consumed, terminated at the altar, they went before God to pray according
to their natural man. Consequently, not only their prayers
were not accepted by God, but even they themselves were
struck dead by God. Hence, everyone who learns to pray must
not only be redeemed by the blood, but he must also be one
who has been terminated and has become ashes. His natural
life has been completely terminated by the cross.

The two aspects of the cross are really not hard to understand, since the types in the Old Testament are displayed
there as clear pictures. We see that no one could enter into
the Holy Place to burn incense and pray to God except by the
blood and the fire from the outside altar. If anyone were to go
into the Holy Place to burn the incense without the fire that
has burned the sacrifice on the altar, he would surely meet
the same fate as Nadab and Abihu. So, without the blood
and the fire, no one could enter into the presence of God.
Without the redemption and the termination of the cross, no
one can have access to God. A man may be able to pray a great
deal before God, but he should not be over-confident that all
his prayers are acceptable to God. The story of Nadab and
Abihu is an excellent case in point. Never merely consider,
"Oh, didn't we pray before God?" No! You still need to ask,
"what about the redemption and termination of the cross?"
Unless you are in the experience of these two aspects of the
cross, you will have no way to go before God.

In today's degraded and deviant Christianity, the common concept is that God answers all our prayers. Yes, brothers and sisters, God is a God Who answers prayers. Yet even more often, He is a God who does not answer prayer. Today many often say, "Please pray for me." This is the slogan of a great number of Christians today. You may see someone coming out of a dance-hall, yet telling you, "Pray for me!" She may be wearing fashionable clothes and be painted with various colors. You may see someone getting ready to attend a Christmas Eve's party. Upon leaving, she may tell a friend, "Please pray for me." Do you think God will answer such prayers? Never! Oh, do not be confident that God will answer all our prayers. Many times our prayers before God not only are not answered, but in His eyes may constitute sinning against Him. We have seen how strictly God dealt with the priests when the tabernacle was first set up and the priests went in before God to offer the sacrifice. If God dealt with the church today in the same way, many would not only suffer spiritual death, but even physically die before God.

In the beginnings of various matters, God was very strict in order to underscore the principle as an iron-clad law. At the time of Pentecost, Ananias and Sapphira lied to the Holy Spirit and fell dead before God. That did not mean that thereafter anyone who lied to the Spirit would fall dead. Later many lied yet did not fall dead. However, in God's sight they had met their death. Nadab and Abihu fell dead because they violated the principles of the cross. To this day, many are still praying in violation of the principle of the cross. Their end is the same. Not only are their prayers not acceptable to God, but they themselves are disapproved of by Him. Their unanswered prayers and God's disapproval are the same in principle as the suffering of physical death in the Old Testament time. Being against God's principle, they suffer God's opposition.

II. THE REDEMPTION OF THE CROSS

The more you are a praying one, the more you will feel that you are sinful, and realize the need for redemption. For example, we can see this condition in Daniel. One of his prayers is recorded in Daniel, chapter nine. In that prayer he made very little mention of the thing that he prayed for. On the contrary, most of that prayer was his confession, not only of his own sins, but also those of the whole nation of Israel. He really understood what it means to pray before God by the blood of the sacrifice of the sin offering.

If a brother or sister does not confess sins at all in a prayer, it is doubtful whether he has entered the presence of God. One who has no consciousness of sins is not only outside the Holy Place, but most likely has not even entered the outer court. He is still outside the white linen hangings. Otherwise, he could not refrain from confessing his sins. This is what is spoken of in 1 John, chapter one: God is light, and if we have fellowship with God and dwell in the light, we will inevitably see our own sins and receive the blood of Jesus, the Son of God, to cleanse us.

Real experiences of prayer are just like this. Whenever you come into the presence of God, you need to experience the redemption of the cross and the cleansing of the blood. The more deeply you enter the presence of God, the more you need to experience the redemption of the cross and the cleansing of the blood. The more deeply you enter the presence of God, the keener your consciousness is of sin, and the deeper your knowledge is concerning sin. Some things in the past that you may have considered to be virtues and merits, you now see as sins. At such a time you tell God, "O God, I can only come into your presence to pray under the blood of Your Son and with the blood of Your Son. Otherwise, I can't even come here, let alone pray." Always realize that whenever you pray you need to experience the redemption of the cross. Otherwise you are filthy, unclean, and full of offense.

One thing is certain: if the Spirit is going to pray through you concerning an important matter, He will first come to enlighten you and to purge your being. Whenever the Spirit is going to bring you into prayer with Him, He needs to purify you once more. And His purification is to first show you your sins and trespasses, and then lead you to receive the cleansing of the blood. Under the precious blood you confess your sins one by one to God. You may confess for an hour and conclude with only five minutes of asking. You need to confess your sins thoroughly until you are without fear and are pure and light inside. Then you can pray, saying, "O, God, the church has a problem here, the work has a difficulty here, etc. I place all these before You."

Even in our giving of thanks and praises during the Lord's table, we should experience the redemption of the cross. Before you go into the Lord's presence to worship and remember Him, you need to go to the cross. No one can go into the Holy Place without going to the altar. You cannot say, "Oh, a few days ago I passed through the altar, so today I can simply walk straight in." If you do so, you will fall into spiritual death before God. Although you confessed your sins yesterday and again this morning when you prayed, you still need to confess your sins this afternoon when you pray. And it is useless to confess with mere empty words. You need to have the consciousness of sins. Whenever a person touches God, he will definitely have the consciousness of sin. When Peter saw the Lord Jesus perform a miracle, thus manifesting Himself as God, immediately he said, "Depart from me; for I am a sinful man, O Lord" (Luke 5:8). It is here that redemption is necessary. We are not able at any time to stand before God by ourselves, but by the redeeming blood of the cross.

III. THE TERMINATION OF THE CROSS

One who knows how to pray and can pray is always one who has been both redeemed under the blood and terminated on the cross. In going before God to pray, first you need to ask whether or not you have been terminated. Suppose you wish to pray concerning the gospel, your family, the giving of material things, or about the matter of marriage. In each case, you need to ask if you have been terminated in that particular matter. You must ask whether you are praying with any self-interest. Whatever you pray for, you need to have a termination in that matter.

Always keep in mind that the fire that burns on the offering altar is the same fire that burns incense on the incense altar. Only the fire that burns the sacrifice into ashes can be the fire that burns the incense. If, without having burned the sacrifice into ashes, the fire is brought to the incense altar to burn the incense, that is called strange fire. You can realize the seriousness of this matter by the fate of Nadab and Abihu. If you have not been terminated in a certain matter, yet you bring that matter into the presence of God in prayer, it is a great offense to God.

Strictly speaking, if one has not been terminated by the cross in a certain matter, it is really not possible for him to pray for that matter. If you have not been terminated by the cross concerning your husband or wife, then, frankly speaking, you are not qualified to pray for your husband or wife. Why is it that many times the Lord does not hear our prayers for our own families? The answer is that we have not become ashes. Those prayers were merely natural prayers, prayers of strange fire. Many times when we pray for the church of God and for the work of the Lord, the Lord does not answer. You pray for the Lord's blessings, yet you do not see the blessings. You have been praying for years, asking the Lord to make the church grow, but the church still has no growth. Your prayers have not been answered because they are prayers of strange fire, natural prayers.

We always have the concept that God will surely hear our prayers because He is merciful and gracious to us. This concept is erroneous. God often does not hear men's prayers. The reason He does not hear is that we, the praying ones, have not passed through the altar. Some bring with them only the blood of the altar, but not the fire. They pass through the redemption, but not through the termination of the altar.

Please remember, whenever man goes to burn incense at the incense altar, he must fulfill two basic conditions. He must experience the blood which tells us that all those who come there to pray have been redeemed and cleansed. He must also experience the fire which tells us that all those who come there to pray have been consumed and have become ashes.

Therefore, brothers and sisters, if the light of the Lord shines on you strongly, immediately you will not be able to pray for a great number of things. The decrease in the number of your prayers proves that you are being purified. If you recognize that many prayers are prayers of strange fire, you will see that those prayers are neither necessary nor right. You will not dare pray those prayers which are for yourself and not for God's sake because they are initiated by you, not by God. After you have been terminated by the cross there is a great purification of your prayer.

Some may ask, "As we have thus been terminated, why do we need to even consider praying? Since we have become ashes that neither speak nor think, everything has been terminated. What more, then, do we need to pray about?" Ashes do mean that everything has been terminated. Do not forget, however, that the fire that burns the ashes is still there to burn the incense before God. When we studied the Old Testament types we became clear that the incense refers to the Lord's resurrection and the fragrance of the Lord in His resurrection. Where the Lord is, there is resurrection. Wherever you and I have been terminated, there is the manifestation of Christ. We first pass through the redemption of the cross before God, accept the termination of the cross, and truly become ashes before God. Then, immediately, Christ becomes the incense which we burn before God.

Strictly speaking, therefore, prayer is both Christ Himself and the expression of Christ. A prayer that is good, right, proper, true, and acceptable to God is the expression of Christ. If you are terminated on the cross, Christ will live out of such a termination. In the case of prayer, Christ is lived out in the prayer. In the case of living, the resurrected Christ is the living. In the ministry, the resurrected Christ is the ministry. Only such a prayer can be acceptable before God and be considered a prayer of sweet-smelling savor. This is a prayer of one who has passed through the cleansing of the blood and the termination of the fire, thus allowing Christ to come forth from within.

Hence, brothers, if you really have a vision of this, you will prostrate yourself before God, confessing your filthiness and your naturalness. You will not be able initially to utter any other prayer. You will see the need to be cleansed by the blood and consumed by the fire. You will say to God, "I am an unclean person, and I am also a natural man. To this day I am still in my natural self. I need Your blood to cleanse me and Your fire to consume me. I need the cross to redeem and also to terminate me." Brothers, when you thus allow the cross to terminate you, you can, in a practical way, experience Christ coming forth from you. It is this resurrected Christ Who becomes your prayer, the incense which you burn before God. You may not pray many prayers, but those that you do pray will be answered by God.

IV. INCENSE BEING ADDED TO PRAYER

Revelation 8 clearly shows us two things: the prayers of the saints, and the Angel, that is, the Lord Jesus, bringing much incense. The incense refers to the resurrected Christ. This incense is added to the prayers of the saints.

May I ask you, brothers and sisters, can the Lord Jesus add the incense to all your prayers? No. If you wish to have the Lord Jesus in resurrection added to your prayer, your prayer surely must pass through the redemption of the blood and the termination of the cross. The prayers in Revelation 8 were prayers of death and resurrection, so once the incense of those prayers was presented before God, there were immediately thunders and lightnings poured down on earth. This means that God both hears and answers those prayers of ours which are in death and resurrection.

Revelation 8 shows us how God in His administration is going to judge this age. But this judgment is waiting for the prayers of those who have received both the redemption of the blood and the termination by the cross. It is waiting for the prayers of those who have been resurrected to seek after His heart and who stand on the position of death, thus allowing the resurrected Christ to be joined with their prayers. Those, thence, will be tremendous prayers which can judge and end this age. We repeat, the reason that they are able to pray for such high and great things is because they have been terminated at the cross and are able to allow the resurrected Christ to be added to their prayers. This is the meaning of the incense being added to the prayers.

We have said before that true prayers are Christ in us praying to the Christ in heaven. Here, then, we have a problem. As we are men of many opinions, how can Christ find a way to come out of our prayers? To allow Him the way, we need to pass through the cleansing of the blood and the termination of the fire. Terminated ones have no opinions. At the cross we receive redemption and termination. Then the Christ in us can be united with us and put us on to pray. Consequently, your prayer is Christ. When Christ thus expresses Himself through us, that is the incense being added to our prayers.

Some say that the incense here refers to the merits of Christ. This is so, but it refers even more to the resurrected Christ. It includes His merits, all that He is, all that He has accomplished, and all that He does. The resurrected Christ with all His work and fruits is the incense. As long as we receive the redemption of the blood and are in the termination of the cross, the Christ in us is joined with us. Then when we pray, it is Christ who prays. At such a time our prayer is the expression of Christ. As a result, before God these prayers are the incense which is acceptable to God and will be answered by God.

Prayers before God must be of two aspects. They include man's prayer, and the incense of Christ's resurrection added to that prayer. In Revelation 5 there are only the prayers of the saints—only the golden bowls with no incense added to them. Therefore, there is also no answer to prayer. Answers to prayer are based on the fact that incense has been added to that prayer. In chapter eight there is a complete picture. There are the prayers of the saints, and there is also the resurrected Christ added as incense to those prayers. Both are being offered before God. At the same time, there are also the answers to prayer being poured down. This is the ultimate result of prayer based on the experience of the cross.

CHAPTER FOURTEEN

LIFE SUPPLY AND PRAYER

I. THE SIGNIFICATION OF THE OLD TESTAMENT TYPE

We place this chapter after the chapter on "The Cross and Prayer" on the basis of the procedure in the tabernacle. When the priest would go in to the incense altar to burn incense, he had to first pass through the offering altar. By this we have seen the relationship between the cross and prayer. After passing through the offering altar and coming into the Holy Place, we find there two items of furniture in addition to the incense altar. There is the table of showbread, followed by the golden lampstand. The showbread and the golden lampstand are for the incense altar. In other words, whoever goes before God to burn the incense must first set the showbread upon the table and keep the lamps of the lampstand in order. Keeping the lamps in order is a matter of life illumination, which we will deal with in the next chapter. In this chapter we will first look at life supply and prayer, that is, the relationship between the showbread table and the incense altar.

The type of the tabernacle in the Old Testament shows us that the showbread table and the incense altar are related. It also reveals to us that all those who burn incense at the incense altar eat of the holy sacrifice upon the offering altar. We know that the holy things refer to Christ Himself being food to those who serve God. All those who burn incense at the incense altar are dependent on the holy things of the offering altar to be their supply. In addition, they should not neglect the aspect of the showbread while they are in the Holy Place. When they burn the incense, not only do they depend on the sacrifice for their food; they are also very much dependent upon the showbread. The holy sacrifice and the showbread being placed before God show forth the fact that the priest's going before God to burn the incense, to pray, is related to life supply. Therefore, if we really want to understand what it means to pray before God in the Holy Place, we must know the supply of the holy sacrifice and the showbread. We must know the relationship between life supply and prayer.

The types clearly indicate to us that everyone who burns incense must take the offerings as their food and have the showbread set before God. Anyone who does not eat the sacrifice properly and anyone who does not have the showbread to bring into the Holy Place shall not be able to burn incense at the incense altar. These two aspects of life supply—one on the inside and the other on the outside—are prerequisites to our prayer. Hence, one who prays before God must take in Christ as his life supply day by day.

II. THE LIFE OF PRAYER

In chapter four we have specifically covered the life of prayer. The life of the new creation which we have received possesses numerous characteristics and innate abilities. One of these many characteristics and innate abilities is prayer. We all know that whenever we are able to pray we feel comfortable within; but whenever we are unable to pray we feel imprisoned, uncomfortable, and unnatural. This means that the characteristic and innate ability of the life in us demands us to pray. If we allow this ability to be expressed, it will lead us spontaneously into prayer, and we will thus feel at ease. But if our situation does not allow this life to spontaneously lead us into prayer, we will sense a condition of being bound. I believe that the children of God have this kind of experience to some extent. This sense of being bound when we fail to pray and feeling at ease when we do pray proves that the life of the new creation within us is a praying life.

III. THE PRAYER OF LIFE

All real prayers are prayers of life. A prayer of life means that such a prayer comes entirely out of life. Because it comes out of life, it is therefore a real prayer. Any prayer that is not of life is feigned, imitated, reluctant, ritual, and outward. In other words, it is false.

Let us assume we have two guests visiting us. One is old, over sixty years of age, and the other is young, a little over two. As we are together, I notice that there is a tremendous difference between our guests in their words and manners. Sometimes the old one tries to copy the smile of the young one. Such a smile is pretentious, false. At other times the young one tries to imitate the language of the old one and sounds somewhat like him. However, there is still the sense that the child is feigning the speech of another. He is not yet sixty years old, but he speaks the words of a sixty-year-old. Although he fakes it very well, you still have to admit that it is false, because his life has not yet reached that stage. If he were to scream and yell, turn the plates upside-down, and throw away the bowls, one would feel that his behavior is genuine, for that behavior genuinely reflects his level of life.

Please keep in mind that the same is true with respect to prayer. A genuine prayer is definitely of life. There is no way to imitate the tone, sound, words, form, and style of the prayers of anyone else. And even if you could imitate them very well, it would still be false.

Brothers and sisters, I hope you can see that prayer is a matter of life. We may not be so strict concerning other matters, but prayer is uniquely and absolutely a matter of life. The extent of your life determines the extent of your prayer. The measure of your life decides the measure of your prayer. Your life is the deciding factor of your prayer. The condition of your life reveals the condition of your prayer. If there is a problem with your life, there will surely be a problem with your prayer. Life and prayer are entirely in direct proportion to one another, and they run parallel to each other. All genuine prayers are prayers of life.

We have said that prayer depends also on words. But do not forget that words are the expression of the degree of one's life. You need to reach a certain degree of life in order to speak the words of that degree. Otherwise, you may have learned to speak them, but they carry neither the backing of

life nor the weight of life. We should not merely exercise ourselves in prayer yet ignore the matter of the growth in life. If
we ignore the growth in life, our prayer will be little different
from a performance. Hence, we need to measure our prayer by
our growth in life. This is an absolute principle.

IV. SUPPLY OF LIFE

The measure of life supply being received by us determines the weightiness of our prayer. One who has the life
supply may not pray with all his life supply, but one who does
not have the life supply cannot possibly pray. In other words,
life supply always exceeds prayer, but prayer can never
exceed life supply.

Do not think that preaching is very hard and praying is
very easy. If you pray in an acting or performing way, then, of
course, it is very easy. But it is not an easy matter to pray a
prayer of burden, a genuine prayer, a prayer that can touch
the throne. Prayer is a difficult labor. According to the histor-
ical record of the human race, there has never been one who
labored on something to the point of sweating blood. But in
the garden of Gethsemane there was One Who did pray and
sweat blood. When Moses prayed on top of the hill, he needed
Aaron and Hur to support his hands. To lift up the hands is
easy, but to lift up the hands and pray is not easy.

Brothers, I know no passage in the Bible that says we
need to fast and preach the Word, but I have certainly found
it to say we need to fast and pray. What does the Bible mean
when it says to fast and pray? It does not mean just to treat
our body severely. It means to exercise our whole being to
bear the burden of a certain matter. Then the burden presses
us to the point that we do not feel hungry, causing us to fast
and pray.

Prayer can supply as well as consume life. On the one
hand, prayer can really cause one to receive supply. On the
other hand, prayer can also cause one to be consumed in life
to a considerable extent. If a prayer does not supply you with
life, that prayer is questionable. On the other hand, if a
prayer does not consume you in life, it is also very questionable. Only those prayers which are a performance do not

consume life. A genuine prayer that bears a burden will definitely be life-consuming. After praying thus for an hour, you need the replenishment of a large measure of life.

Therefore, one who seeks true prayer should know how to obtain the life supply. Many times when we draw near to the Lord it is not to pray but to fellowship with Him in order to gain some life supply. To pray in a genuine way, one should not bear too many burdens daily; otherwise, it will become a real hardship and suffering. Because prayer is the highest as well as the most lasting part of spiritual work, it really consumes life. We should not overwork ourselves, and in the same principle, we should not pray excessively. This means that our prayer must not exceed the life supply. Everyday we should have a time when we do not bear any burden of prayer but merely draw near to the Lord and receive His supply.

I hope that every brother and sister will remember this principle: if you do not receive the supply of life at set times daily, your prayer is certainly questionable. If there is no life supply, there is definitely no prayer life. Hence, we must learn to receive the supply of Christ as life continually. Receive the supply of life through the quiet time, meditation, calling on the Lord, reading the Word, and through fellowshipping with the saints. This will enable us to have true prayers before God. We also need to learn to receive the burden in prayer. However, it must not be too heavy a burden lest we suffer loss. Receive regular life supply daily; this is a great principle of prayer.

V. DEALINGS OF LIFE

It is very hard to always maintain our life before the Lord in a trouble-free condition. Usually, and unconsciously, our life within incurs some problems. Once this happens, immediately we are not able to pray. For example, you may have a controversy with the Lord regarding a certain matter. You refuse to obey the Lord's will. Rather, you insist on acting according to your own will. Once such a controversy exists, there is a problem in your life, and you cannot pray. Even if you do pray, your prayers are not real. You must resolve this controversy by saying to the Lord, "Lord, I will let You win again in this matter. I am willing to be defeated by You." At this point the prayer in you can be restored.

It is not only controversies that cause problems in life. Even speaking a few unnecessary words in our daily life can affect our prayer. Hence, we must deal strictly with all the things that may affect our prayer. We must always adjust the condition of our inner life.

Nothing restricts and controls man more severely than prayer. If you do not pray for a week, you will surely be very far from the Lord and become completely loose. One who prays much every day is, without question, fully restricted. You may do as you please in everything but prayer. For example, the Lord's teaching shows us that when we pray we need to forgive others. Whenever we do not forgive others, we cannot pray. It is because of this that some, at times, have been unable to pray. Although they may sometimes speak words of prayer, they know very well that they are not really before the throne of God. They know that there is a separation, a distance, between them and God, for they have not been able to forgive their brother. This means their life has incurred some problem. Hence, you need to learn the lessons of prayer by dealing with your inner life. You will notice that you not only will be able to learn a great deal in prayer, but you will have daily growth in life. No other activity requires the supply of life more than prayer. Neither is there anything else that can cause a Christian to grow faster than prayer.

VI. LIVING IN LIFE

To learn to pray, we must learn first to continually live in life and not depart from it. We need to follow the consciousness of life and live in the fellowship of life. Whenever we depart from life, we have no way to pray. Those who pray the most and who are the most thorough and weighty in prayer are those who continually live in life. The lesson of prayer is absolutely a spiritual matter, a matter of life. Regardless how much you have learned, it always involves the spirit and revolves around life. All the lessons of life are here in the spirit. Therefore, if we wish to learn the lessons of prayer, we need to be one who lives in life.

For example, let us consider a gospel meeting in the church. When you attend such a meeting there are several possibilities. You may feel that since this is the church preaching the gospel, it is imperative that you, as a brother or sister serving God, participate. Therefore you attend the meeting. Another possibility may be that the elders keep telling you that this gospel preaching really needs you, and it is imperative that you come. Then, feeling you have no choice, you come. Please remember, these are not examples of living in life. And since your reason for attending is not in life, you are not able to offer much prayer for this matter. The situation should be such that in your spirit you feel very much concerned for the gospel preaching. Then, spontaneously, you will be able to pray. Hence, brothers, in order to pray you need to learn to live in life in every matter.

The same is true concerning the relationships you have with the brothers and sisters. You may have various reasons to maintain your relationship with the brothers and sisters. But unless those reasons are in life, they can never cause you to pray for the brothers and sisters. You and I need to learn severe lessons and condemn anything that is not life. How do you know what is of life? You have to ask whether there is prayer or not. If your relationship with the brothers and sisters is of life, you will pray a great deal. It is not because the brothers or sisters ask you to pray for them. It is because your relationship with them is of life, so you cannot keep from praying for them. If it is not of life, even if you intend to pray, you will not feel the urgency in your inner being. Hence, you will simply forget it after a time.

Therefore, please remember: where life is, there is prayer; where life is not, there is no prayer. If we do not live in life, even our prayer for our relatives cannot last long. We can only pray once, and that is all. Only in life can there be the real, lasting prayers.

Brothers, learn therefore, to live in life. We must admit that there are not many praying ones in our midst, and a number of brothers and sisters have a problem in their prayer life. The reason there is inadequate prayer is that there is a problem in life. Whenever there is a problem with life, there is also a problem concerning prayer. Hence, in order to pray, one needs to learn to always live in life. Studying, discussing, exhorting, encouraging, and solving problems are futile when there are not the genuine prayers. Only by learning to live in life can one have real prayers.

Take, for example, a local church that is having problems. You may, with all good intentions, wish to be a peacemaker to straighten out their problems by ironing out all their different concepts and ideas, thus making them one. These methods, being apart from life, are useless, and you would not have much real prayer. There is only one way for you to have real prayers that touch the throne regarding the problems of the church. That way is to live in life. The solution to the problems of the church hinges on your prayer. When there is the prayer of life, the problem is solved. Unless you live in life, your prayer will surely not last long, cannot be sincere, and is therefore useless.

Why is it that whenever certain ones pray for the gospel, immediately some souls get saved, while others pray continually, yet none get saved? The reason hinges on whether or not the praying ones are living in life. Some have told us, "You should go and work among a certain people!" Brothers and sisters, you may say this a thousand times, but it is still useless. Instead, we need men who live in life in all things. It is not a matter of having a natural view or making an ordinary observation, but a matter of learning to live in life. The result will be some real prayers in life. Such prayers are of the Lord, and they will be effective. Otherwise, regardless how hard you try to promote a matter, it is in vain.

All genuine prayers, prayers that touch the throne, issue from life. Please forgive me. I have seen many problems of the brothers and sisters in different localities, but I seldom pray for them, because I am short of life concerning those places. In other words, I do not have the capacity to take the burden. To take the burden means that in that particular matter you live in life. To make intercession is not an easy, light matter. It is not that I tell you, "Brother, please pray for such-and-such a church," and you reply, "Okay." Then as soon as you go home you kneel down and pray, "O Lord, have pity

on the church there." This is useless. And there will not
be much prayer, anyway. Maybe after praying two or three
times, you simply forget about it. And maybe after a month,
you even forget that you have prayed for that particular
matter.

To have genuine prayers means that you are able to take
this matter into your life. It should be that while you contact
that backsliding church, by touching the inner fellowship and
consciousness, you are convinced that the Lord has placed the
burden of the problem of that church in you. And, as you have
this consciousness in you, you utter some kind of prayer. That
kind of prayer you cannot forget, because if you do not pray,
you bear a burden and do not feel relieved. Rather, you feel
pressed and burning within. This kind of prayer is of life.

May the Lord cover me with His blood—I very much dislike a common saying in Christianity: "Please pray for me."
One day while I was at the airport for someone's departure, I
noticed some very modern, fashionable, and up-to-date people
whose conversation and action produced an atmosphere that
made others feel very uncomfortable. But when the time came
for them to shake hands and say goodbye, they still could say
to one another, "Please pray for me." When I heard that, I felt
nauseated. In Christianity this is a conventional phrase
which is of little use. Every true prayer comes out of life.
Anyone who is not in life surely is unable to pray.

In the Old Testament, Daniel was a praying one who lived
in life, and that life was his prayer. Read those prayers of
Daniel, and you can see that they were all in life. His living
and his life were such that he could have prayers which were
weighty before God. Likewise, after the Lord's ascension, the
one hundred and twenty prayed ten days and brought forth
the outpouring of the Holy Spirit on the day of Pentecost.
Many people bring up this matter today and encourage others
to pray like them. But what is the use of such encourage-
ment? You need to realize that they were able to pray for ten
consecutive days because they lived that kind of life. The
prayers of the Lord Jesus in the Gospels were also according
to the same principle. He often went up to the mountain to
pray because He lived that kind of life.

Prayer is altogether a matter of life. Hence, to learn the lessons of prayer, one needs to learn the lessons of life. Learn to have more dealings and adjustments in the matters of life Also learn to live in life and take the burden of life. Thus, there will be no need for others to exhort you to pray. You will spontaneously pray. The amount of real prayer one has is definitely determined by the measure of life within him.

CHAPTER FIFTEEN

LIFE ILLUMINATION AND PRAYER

In the previous two chapters we have covered the relationship between the cross and prayer and the relationship between life supply and prayer. In this chapter we shall continue by speaking about the relationship between life illumination and prayer. These three chapters are related on the basis of the service of the Old Testament priests burning the incense in the Holy Place. Keep in mind that in the Old Testament types, when the priests entered the Holy Place to burn the incense, they had to pass through the altar of burnt offering. After getting into the Holy Place, they first placed the showbread on its table. Second, they dressed the lamps, and finally, they burned the incense. Hence, passing through the altar, the table of the showbread, and the lampstand is absolutely related to the burning of the incense before God. Everyone who goes before God to burn the incense must pass through these three places in his experience. The cross and prayer speak of the relationship between the altar of burnt offering and the incense altar. Life supply and prayer speak of the relationship between the showbread table and the incense altar. Life illumination and prayer are concerned with the relationship between the lampstand and the incense altar.

I. THE SIGNIFICATION OF THE OLD TESTAMENT TYPE

The priests going to the golden altar to burn the incense had to pass through the altar of offerings. They also had to pass through the showbread table and the lampstand. This means that everyone who goes before God to pray must pass through the cross. They must also experience Christ as life to

such an extent that they are able to bring with them the
Christ they have enjoyed and set Him before God. They must
also experience Christ as light to the extent that they become
illuminated within.

We know through experience that the more one draws
near to God, the more he is in the light and becomes illuminated within. This does not mean that after you pray to God
you will become illuminated within. Rather, it means that as
you pass through the cross and enjoy Christ as life, this life
becomes the illuminating light within you. Only such an illuminated one will have incense acceptable to God, and can
therefore go before Him to pray.

No one should go foolishly before God to pray when he is
in a darkened, dim, murky, and gloomy state. If we go before
God in such a state, we will have neither many words nor
much burden to pray. One who is able to go before God to
burn the incense is one who has passed through the altar, has
enjoyed Christ and set Him as the bread before God, has lit
the lamp, and is shining within.

Notice here that if the light of the lampstand were put out
so that the entire Holy Place were dark, there would be no
way for anyone to burn the incense at the golden altar. Being
in darkness, one would not know where to begin. It is entirely
by the light of the lampstand that one is able to move and act
and know what to do at the incense altar. This is a very clear
picture. Many times when we go before God to pray, we have
not lit the lamp and are without light inside. Therefore, we
can only pray foolishly, groping entirely in darkness. Strictly
speaking, if we are in such a situation, we should not even
start to pray. We should first turn within to deal with the
matter of illumination. When you are illuminated and can see
clearly, knowing what and how to pray, you can start praying.

To care for the matter of illumination, we must first
be dealt with at the offering altar. This means that we are
broken by the application of the cross. We now experience
Christ as life and enjoy Him as the showbread. Then according to what we have experienced and enjoyed, we bring Christ
as the food of life and set Him before God for God to appreciate. Then the light within us will surely be shining, for that

life we have experienced is the light. Now when we go before God to pray even for a few minutes, we will feel that we are illuminated within—the lamp within is shining. The Christ Whom we have experienced, Whom we have brought and set before God for His appreciation, is also the light of life that shines in us. At such a point we can easily pray before God. We also are very clear for which things we should or should not pray. We can touch the incense altar and know what we should do there. We know how to burn the incense. All those who have had the experience can testify of this. Hence, life illumination is absolutely related to prayer. Without lighting the lamp, we cannot burn the incense.

II. LIFE ILLUMINATION

The illumination we are referring to is not the result of some kind of instruction in doctrine or teaching in truth. Rather, it is primarily produced by man's subjective experience in life. While the light in the outer court is natural, the light in the Holy Place shines forth as a result of adding the beaten olive oil to the golden lampstand. On the one hand, it is the gold beaten and shaped into a lampstand. On the other hand, it is the oil produced from crushed olives. This is entirely a subjective experience of the inner life. Once you have the practical and subjective experience of the Lord, the life in you will have the function of illumination.

Some messages concerning the truth seem to issue in a kind of enlightenment, making known to men what is pleasing to God and what is not pleasing to God. However, these messages are unable to cause men to burn incense before God in a deeper way. Only the illumination resulting from one's experience in life can enable him to go before God and burn the incense in a deeper way. Hence, real prayers are not the result of keeping the outward doctrines, but of being enlightened by the light of life within. I may give eight or ten messages telling the brothers and sisters to fast and pray. I may speak very logically and with great persuasiveness. But I know that after my speaking, they will not be able to fast and pray, because their doing so would be merely due to the influence of the doctrine. What you must have is an experience before the Lord, so that even though no one has ever taught you anything about the matter of fasting, you cannot help but fast and pray. Then it will be something of your experience in life. There is an inner light shining and compelling you to fast. It is not an outward doctrine but an inward realization that will not let you go. At that time, your fasting and prayer are the issue of the life illumination. Take another example: I may preach the word in Matthew 5 which says, "Therefore, if you are offering your gift at the altar and there remember that your brother has anything against you, leave your gift there before the altar and go away; first be reconciled to your brother, and then come and offer your gift." My message may be merely an outward doctrine and not the illumination of life. You must learn to live in the Lord and experience Him as life. Thus, there will be something in you that keeps enlightening you. If you continue to condemn your brother there will be something in you condemning you. This is the light of life. Only this kind of light can enable you to have real prayers.

As another example, suppose you hear a brother speaking a word concerning how to pray. If you have the experience in life, you will be able to discern whether his exhortation is just an outward doctrine or is from his inner experience. If it is an outward doctrine, you may become greatly stirred, but it will produce no result. But if it is his own experience, then his word will be able to open and touch your inner being. While you are listening, the light in you is mysteriously lit. You feel that there is something in you shining and pressing you so that when you go home you cannot help but pray.

I hope that the brothers and sisters will learn the deep lessons in these matters. Then when they stand up to give a word, that word will be able to touch the inner being of men. It will cause them to have a kind of life function issuing forth as an illumination, so that under the illumination of life they will spontaneously pray.

Only those who experience the illumination of life are able to receive the burden and commission before God and bear the burden in prayer. Many times in their prayers they almost forget themselves. They remember very little concerning their own needs or problems—whether in the material aspect, the business aspect, or even the spiritual aspect. Such a person may have a certain weakness that he is unable to overcome, but he does not pay much attention to it. The more one cares for himself, praying and dealing with his own weaknesses, the more it proves that he may not be in the light nor living in the experience of life. One who lives in the experience of life, and thus in the light, will pray largely outside himself. He is able to receive a definite burden which is not the result of some outward exhortation, but the issue of the inner illumination of life.

III. THE WORK OF THE LIGHT OF LIFE
ON THE NEGATIVE SIDE

It is a certainty that the most purified person is the one who can pray the most effectively. If you ask me, "Who are the most purified ones in the universe?" I would reply, "They are those who can pray the most effectively." The degree of your competency in prayer before God is determined by the degree of your purity. The more competent you are in prayer, the more evident it is that you are living in the light of life.

The light of life working in us always starts on the negative side. It shines and fixes itself upon us, not merely enlightening us on the surface, but much more, penetrating deeply into us. It is as if the light is able to split open our inner parts. This light penetrating into our depths not only exposes every little error in our action and attitude but touches the very root of our being. It touches our motive, our intention, the depths of our spirit, and the very source of all that issues from us. It can reveal whether or not our spirit is calm and pliable. Although we may not be wrong, unclean, or sinful outwardly, we may still be neither calm nor pliable inwardly. Once the light of life shines on these things, they are immediately exposed.

Everyone who truly learns to pray before God must be enlightened, and he must deal with himself severely under such a light. It is in such a light of life that we are able to learn deep, fine, and valuable lessons before the Lord. Our experience tells us that this penetrating light will illuminate us to a point where we feel that there is no place in the universe for us to hide. Then, and only then, can we know what it means to have nothing to be proud of or to boast about. Only then do we appreciate the fact that our only place of refuge is His precious blood. Our intention, our motive, our purpose, the spirit within, the inner source, will all be made manifest by the light. When the light illuminates, there are a number of feelings and experiences which are simply indescribable with human words. Hence, brothers and sisters, prayer is not a matter of how many answers you have obtained or how much faith you have. Rather, it is a matter of how much you live in the illumination of life.

Many praise Brother Müller, who established orphanages and had 1,500,000 prayers answered in his lifetime. Many praise him as a man of faith. However, when I read Müller's diaries, I was not as impressed by his faith as by the fact that he lived entirely in the illumination of God. My first impression was not that he had great faith, but that here was a man who whenever he went before God was scrutinized by God. As God scrutinized and illuminated him, he uttered some prayers under the shining light. Spontaneously, it was very easy for him to have faith and equally easy for his prayers to be answered by God.

In prayer, therefore, faith is not the most important matter. The first thing to learn is to be worked on by the illumination of life. You must allow it to expose you to the extent that nothing in your being remains hidden. Even you yourself have no place in which to hide. For in the light you have discovered that your whole being is a problem. There is no way for you to burn the incense before God because your inner condition is not right. At this point you know that your only place of refuge is the blood which was shed on the cross. It is here that, in a practical way, you experience the preciousness of the blood. And then by your experience you really know the meaning of the words in 1 John chapter one. You know what it means when it says that God is light, and what it means to have fellowship with God. You know what it means to be cleansed by the blood of Jesus, the Son of God. This is the first aspect of the work of the life illumination in us.

Please remember that all those who are competent in prayer are those who prostrate themselves before God. This prostration is entirely due to the illumination. Before men you may be proud and unwilling to throw yourself to the ground, but you cannot help but prostrate yourself before God. Such prostrating is not merely being knocked down by God outwardly or being subdued by God's environmental discipline, but it is the inner illumination that has prostrated you. Strictly speaking, God's environmental discipline still cannot prostrate you. It is always the light's illuminating that prostrates you. (Of course, some also need the help of the outward discipline.) Consequently, you discover that your only trust is in the blood, and thus you become one who is prostrated to the ground. Your entire being has no escape before God, and you can only hide yourself under the blood. Thus, you are able to pray.

IV. THE WORK OF THE LIGHT OF LIFE
ON THE POSITIVE SIDE

When we live in the light of life, there are always two aspects to its work in us. On the negative side, it deals with us, scrutinizes, penetrates, exposes, purges, subdues, and ultimately, prostrates us. On the positive side, it causes us to have the burden, guidance, words, and utterance for prayer. Such burden, guidance, words, and utterance for prayer are the result of the shining of the light of life in us. This shining in us is the anointing of the ointment in us. Once you have the positive work of the illumination, learn to bring your whole being to a halt and pray before God according to that illumination. Do not care too much for the needs in the outward environment nor for the items of prayer in your memory. Pray according to whatever the illumination shines on and anoints in you.

Brothers, only those who have learned the lessons of prayer can know what is meant by "the wind blows where it wills." Only such ones know what is meant by being able to move freely. At this point you can somewhat understand how the big wheel in Ezekiel chapter one completely follows the movements of the spirit. Wherever the spirit goes, the big wheel goes.

You do not make a decision to pray for such-and-such a work, such-and-such a person, or such-and-such a church. Rather, you pray entirely according to the moving of the spirit within. The spirit within blows like the wind. All you need to do is follow its blowing.

Take the prayers of Daniel as examples, and you will see that the Holy Spirit worked in him positively as well as negatively. You can see that Daniel was a man who prostrated himself before God. In doing so he represented both himself and the entire people of Israel. Having allowed the light of life to thus work in him, he began to utter positive prayers before God. He could cry out to God: "O our God...cause thy face to shine upon thy sanctuary...for the Lord's sake...O Lord, hearken and do; defer not, for thine own sake..." (Dan. 9:17, 19). See how this kind of prayer touches great heights and depths! This is what we mean by the positive work of the light of life in us.

Brothers, I believe that many among us need to enter into this lesson of prayer. We may tell the new believers, "On Monday, pray for your relatives and friends; Tuesday, for the church; Wednesday, for the gospel; and Thursday, for the work abroad." It may not be wrong to tell new believers to pray in this way as an initial exercise, but our experience tells us that these fixed prayers will gradually become dead prayers. The more you pray this way, the more you become dead, the emptier you are within, the less you touch reality, and the worse you feel within. Hence, we need to learn to be enlightened by life. Whenever we go before God to burn the incense, we must learn to have something to set upon the showbread table. We must also learn to light and dress the lamps at the lampstand. On the negative side we need to prostrate ourselves under the illumination. On the positive side we need to allow the light to anoint us with what God desires and what He wants to accomplish. Then these will become our burden and leading. This illumination and anointing will give us the words and the utterance to pray before God.

Read the prayer in Daniel chapter nine, and you will have to admit that Daniel was a man who not only had the burden, but also the utterance to pray. Consider what he prayed:

"O our God...cause thy face to shine upon thy sanctuary...for the Lord's sake." His word, his expression, was really full of such utterance that God could not help but be touched. That word was able to bind God and compel Him to act. That prayer was uttered not just because someone desired to pray before God. Rather, it was that such a man having been illuminated within, prostrated himself before God, and, at the same time, received the positive burden, guidance, words, and utterance from God. Then he prayed according to the inner shining. Hence, such prayer was valuable and weighty before God.

We all need to learn to stop the activity of our being, our self. We must not allow our decision, memory, outward needs, or clamorings to disturb the positive work of the light of life within us. We should only pray before God according to what we see and feel under the positive shining of the light in us.

V. THE REST THAT RESULTS FROM LIFE ILLUMINATION

As we touch the work of the life illumination on the positive side and pray accordingly, at a certain time we will surely become very restful within. Such rest cannot be explained by the mind. It is entirely something deep in the spirit. Many times, although we are disturbed and attacked in our mind and are miserable in our emotion, there is an unexplainable rest in the depth of our being. Rationally, the disturbance may be due to some environmental influence or Satan's attack, but we need to believe only in the peace and rest in our depths. One thing is certain: if in accordance with the positive work of the life illumination in you, you speak forth all the burden, leading, words, and utterance which you have felt, then you will surely be full of rest within. Outwardly, you may be attacked and disturbed both mentally and emotionally. Learn to ignore it. Trust only in the inner peace, and thus rest yourself completely. Thus, experience will tell you that not only are you a restful man, but you are also one who is illuminated within. You are transparent, restful, and very shining. In addition, at this point you can discern the inner condition of whomever comes before you. This is a very wonderful thing because you are in the light. You can sense how much of him is shining and how much of him is not shining. This is man's transparent condition resulting from the life illumination in prayer.

May such a picture in the tabernacle be clearly impressed upon us. As the fragrance ascends from the altar of incense, the light at the lampstand is always shining. These two perfectly match and blend with one another. Without exception, every time the fragrance goes up, the light is shining.

Brothers, if you learn the lessons of prayer to this extent, you will surely be shining within. When you pray, you will sense there is the fragrance ascending, and you will feel very restful and at ease. At the same time you will also be in the light and will feel transparently clear. Hence, we need to learn to live in the light so that we can truly be men of prayer.

Concerning the matter of prayer, many of God's children today pay too much attention to receiving answers from their prayers and hope too much to have a living faith. I hope that henceforth we would not esteem these things too highly. Do not care too much whether or not your prayer is answered. Neither pay too much heed to so-called faith. But diligently learn to be illuminated by life. Learn to be enlightened within and dealt with until you prostrate yourself under the shining of the light. Learn also to pray before God in accordance with the positive work of the enlightenment. Pray until you feel at ease and restful within. Then just be at peace. That is good enough. Practice this and you will see that your prayer is acceptable to God, and that you are a peaceful, restful man as well as an illuminated one.

CHAPTER SIXTEEN

THE NECESSITY FOR PRAYER
TO BE IN RESURRECTION

I. THE INDICATION OF THE OLD TESTAMENT TYPE

Beginning with chapter thirteen, we have been dealing with the various aspects of prayer based on the Old Testament types. We have covered the matter concerning the cross and prayer based on the relationship between the offering altar and the incense altar. We have covered the matter of life supply and prayer based on the relationship between the showbread table and the incense altar. Based on the relationship between the golden lampstand and the incense altar, we have also covered the matter of life illumination and prayer. Now, based on the type of the incense altar itself, we shall see the necessity for prayer to be in resurrection.

In spiritual experience, the outer court of the tabernacle denotes the earth, the earthly aspect; whereas, the Holy Place and the Holy of Holies denote the heavens, the heavenly aspect. Whatever is heavenly is in resurrection. The showbread table signifies that the Lord is our bread of life. This is of the heavenly aspect and is, therefore, in resurrection. The golden lampstand indicates that the Lord is our light of life. This is also of the heavenly aspect and in resurrection. The incense altar which denotes man's prayer before God is entirely something in resurrection.

Whenever the Bible speaks of man going before God to burn the incense, it invariably refers to man going before God to pray. For example, in the beginning of the Gospel of Luke, it says that Zacharias, the father of John the Baptist, entered the temple of the Lord to burn incense. Then it refers to the people praying outside at the hour of incense. Also,

Revelation chapters five and eight tell us that the burning of incense before God is the prayer of the saints ascending to God. Therefore, to burn the incense is to pray.

Among the spices that are burnt on the incense altar, the principal one is frankincense. In the Bible, frankincense specifically signifies resurrection, just as myrrh denotes death. The frankincense which is burnt on the incense altar is a symbol of resurrection. When the sweet-smelling savor ascends, there is altogether an atmosphere in resurrection. Hence, according to the type in the Old Testament, man going before God to burn incense is entirely a matter in resurrection. This indicates that man's prayers before God must be in resurrection.

Although we are praying on earth today, strictly speaking, every prayer must be in the position of ascension. And although we who pray are humans, every prayer needs to be in resurrection. For our prayer to be acceptable to God and be considered by God as a sweet-smelling savor, it must be in ascension and in resurrection. There is no burning of incense, no prayer, at the offering altar. All the incense must be burnt at the incense altar. I believe this picture in typology is very clear.

In the tabernacle setting one must pass through the offering altar, the laver, the showbread table, and the lampstand, and then arrive at the incense altar. This entire picture is for one thing: that man may go before God to burn incense, that is, to utter prayers before God by drawing near to God and contacting God. Such prayer is absolutely in resurrection.

II. THE MEANING OF RESURRECTION

What is resurrection, after all? We shall look at it from three aspects:

A. Resurrection Means to Be Raised from Death

Resurrection is a state of having passed completely through death and having risen from death. To be in resurrection is different than to be alive. To be alive is the original state without having passed through death. To be in resurrection is to have passed through death and to have been raised up. That which is not in harmony with God, that which is not of God, and that which cannot last eternally is completely terminated once it goes into death. But that which is of God, compatible with God, and eternally existing can pass through death and emerge in resurrection. Hence, to pray in resurrection means that man should pray not according to himself nor according to his natural being. He should not pray according to those things which cannot remain eternally nor according to those things which are incompatible with God. Rather, he must completely go through the cross, which is to pass through death. Then he will be able to pray in resurrection.

B. Resurrection Is God

In John 11:25, the Lord Jesus says explicitly, "I am the resurrection." God is the resurrection. Even in the Old Testament, God is already the resurrection. Some may ask, "Before the incarnation, in the Old Testament age, how can you say that God is the resurrection?" Please remember, with God there is no time element of before and after. There is only the matter of His eternal nature. God is life, and this life is resurrection.

A certain brother once said something very meaningful. He said, "A grain of sand is finished and cannot come forth after it is buried in the ground. On the other hand, once a seed is buried in the ground and encounters death, it becomes resurrected and breaks forth." This is true. The unbelievers are finished when they go into death. However, Christians should be afraid that they might miss death, for whenever they go into death, the function of the life within them becomes manifest. Unbelievers are afraid of the environment of death, but Christians should welcome it. Whenever Christians fall into death it is an opportunity for them to live by being resurrected. This life, which is God Himself, is resurrection. He never fears death. On the contrary, He welcomes death, because through death He can manifest Himself as resurrection. Now we see what it means to pray in resurrection. To pray in resurrection is to pray in life. It is to pray in

God Who fears not death and to pray in God Who passes through death and still lives.

C. Resurrection Is the Holy Spirit

To be in resurrection also means to be in the Holy Spirit. Once the Lord Jesus entered into the realm of resurrection, He entered into the Holy Spirit. All the experiences which you and I have in the Holy Spirit today are in resurrection. In other words, only those who are in the Holy Spirit are able to touch the reality of resurrection. The Holy Spirit is the reality of resurrection. The Lord Jesus entered into resurrection. To be in resurrection is to be in the Holy Spirit, and to touch the Holy Spirit is to touch resurrection. Praying in resurrection is praying in the Holy Spirit.

Within the resurrected Spirit, there are both the elements of God and the elements of man. This is typified by the incense mentioned in Exodus 30, which is composed of frankincense plus other spices. The anointing oil is also composed of elements representing both God and man. It is very hard to separate the incense from the anointing oil. In the spiritual reality, the reality of the incense is the anointing oil, and the reality of the anointing oil is the incense. In other words, the reality of resurrection is the Spirit, and the Spirit is resurrection itself. To touch the Spirit is to touch resurrection. However, never consider that man is altogether annulled in the experience of prayer. On the contrary, every part of man such as his mind, will, emotion, desires, insight, judgment, and volition may be renewed in the Spirit and be mingled with the prayer in resurrection. The mind of prayer, the emotion of prayer, and the will of prayer, which we have mentioned in the past chapters, are items in resurrection.

Hence, resurrection means that everything of man is terminated and everything of God is manifested. Resurrection is also God being life to man, and it is the very Spirit. To pray in resurrection is to pray in the Spirit. Having understood the meaning of resurrection, we can understand why prayer needs to be in resurrection.

III. PRAYER IN RESURRECTION

Every time we pray before God, we need to deeply experience death and resurrection. For example, you may pray for
the church or for the work of God. If you remain for a time
somewhat quiet before the Lord, you will have an inner realization that there are so many natural and human elements
in your prayer. You will discern the presence of human ideas,
desires, inclinations, choices, and demands. At this time, if
you are careless and negligent, you will feel as if you are
offering a prayer of strange fire or strange incense. This is
not the incense of the sweet spices which God wants. You will
sense that God will not listen. And you will also condemn
yourself within. If you have learned the lessons precisely,
once you come to this point, you will not be able to utter a
word. First you need to pass through the cross. You need the
cross to do a separating and purifying work, so that the natural things may be thoroughly removed. Otherwise, you will
have no way to pray.

When we first got saved, it was very easy for us to open
our mouth before God. It seemed that we were very relaxed
and prayed freely for anything. But gradually, as we learned
the lessons, we could no longer pray for many of these things
before God. Later, as we knelt to pray, we had the inner sensation that in those matters we still had our inclinations,
desires, choices, prejudices, ideas, and biases.

Sometimes we notice that two brothers are at odds with
one another, and we intend to pray for them. But as we are
about to open our mouth, we realize that there is something
not right within us. Our emotion is moved. We have some
prejudice in the matter. Unless we deal with our situation
first, we will not be able to pray before God. Also, in praying
for our material needs, often we discover that we are very
much in ourselves and not in resurrection. Therefore, we
simply cannot utter any words. Such experiences prove that
we have learned a great deal before God.

When those who have not learned the lessons go before
God, they are really daring and are not afraid to pray for anything. I know of someone who went before God and prayed,

"O God, You see how much that person has hurt me; You must stretch out Your hand to give him a heavier blow than he has given me." And some sisters who have been offended by their husbands would pray with weeping and crying, "O Lord, You must vindicate me; You must extend Your hand to deal with my husband." By listening to such prayers, you know those individuals probably have not even entered the gate to the outer court of the tabernacle. That is why they are so daring. If a person has really entered into the Holy Place, touched the altar of incense, and learned some lessons, he would not be able to pray in such a way. Many times he is unable to pray, but can only groan.

Brothers and sisters, I am convinced that when Romans 8:26 says, "The Spirit Himself intercedes for us with groanings which cannot be uttered," it is due to our ignorance of the principle of resurrection. Many times we pray in ourselves, and when the Spirit forbids us within, we do not know how else to pray. Suppose we go to visit a brother who is sick, and we are very clear inside that God's hand is upon him for some reason. But his wife, who is also a sister, naturally hopes that her husband will be quickly healed. At such a time it is very hard for us to pray. Sometimes we would try to do her a favor by praying, "O Lord, You are omnipotent, and You are able to raise the dead. O Lord, Your intention is to give peace and not to send woes; surely You will cause our brother to be healed." While you are praying in this way, you know you are merely trying to please her. Ordinarily, under such circumstances, we have no way to pray. We cannot say, "O Lord, we thank and praise You, for it is You Who are doing a work in this brother." As we do not dare pray in this way, we can only groan. Because we cannot measure up to the principle of death and resurrection, many times the Holy Spirit has to pray with groanings in us. Since we cannot pray for him in either a negative or a positive way, we can only allow the Spirit to intercede in us with groanings which cannot be uttered.

I have met a number of brothers and sisters who prayed boldly for their families, enterprises, and children. The contents of their prayers were nothing but asking for blessings, longevity, and peace. Moreover, they even had the scriptural basis, saying, "O God, You are rich in mercy, and You would never make us suffer. As You have given us Your Son, so there is not one good thing that You would withhold from us." When I was young I could not explain why my inner sense could not agree with this kind of prayer. Gradually, I found out that such prayer was not the burning of incense on the incense altar. Rather, it was a prayer that had not passed through death. It had not been seasoned by experience before the Lord and was uttered carelessly.

We often feel that to pray for certain things would almost be an insult to God. We do not dare to pray in such a way. There is an inner prohibition, an inner condemnation. This comes not because we are told anything by anyone; rather, it comes as a spontaneous feeling within when we are about to pray. As we are about to open our mouth, we feel that in us there are still our desires, our goals, and our selections. Once we feel this way, we do not dare to pray anymore. After such a purification, whatever remains for which one can pray and dares to pray is a prayer in resurrection. This kind of situation varies from person to person. It is not absolute but relative. In any case, the more deeply and strictly you have learned the lessons, the smaller the sphere of what you can pray and dare to pray becomes. One who prays most effectively has the most limited sphere of prayer. Only those who do not know prayer enjoy a broad sphere of prayer. No other place requires us to pass through death and resurrection more absolutely than does the incense altar. This is the requirement of prayer.

I met a brother who when he debates with someone speaks strongly and convincingly. He argues fiercely and feels he is right in everything. But after the debate is over, when everyone begins to pray, his first sentence is a confession, saying, "O Lord, all the words that I have just spoken are an offense to You; do forgive me." Thus, you see, once a man comes to pray, he immediately encounters the requirement of death and resurrection. Not only the words, but even our inner intents and motives are made manifest at the incense altar. Hence, in helping others, we do not need to argue so much. The best thing we can do is to bring them before God. Once

they pray, they know immediately that they are still natural.
They have not passed through death and come into resurrection.

Among the children of God today, there is a very wrong
concept. Some keep telling others that to pray one must have
faith in order that God might answer his prayer. When people
talk about prayer today, immediately they talk about faith.
Brothers and sisters, please understand that faith is not
something which you can have as you will. The most important requirement of prayer is not that you have faith, but that
you are able to pass through the offering altar and arrive at
the incense altar. Prayer is a matter of death and resurrection, not a matter of faith.

Prayer is entirely a matter between the two altars, the
offering altar and the incense altar. Anything that is condemned of God, anything that is incompatible with God, and
anything that cannot last eternally must be dealt with and
terminated at the offering altar. You need to burn the incense
before God with the fire taken from the altar of burnt
offering. It is not necessary to worry about having faith concerning anything that you can pray for. God is your faith.
Surely God will answer any prayer that is in resurrection.
You only need to learn the lesson of death and resurrection
and to pray under that principle. Then you will have the guidance to pray, the words to pray, and the faith of prayer. If you
are in resurrection, you cannot help but believe, and God will
certainly answer your prayer.

Hence, when Romans 8 speaks of prayer, it does not mention the matter of faith at all. It only says that the Holy Spirit
helps us in our weakness, for we do not know for what we
should pray as is fitting, but the Spirit Himself intercedes for
us with groanings which cannot be uttered. The prayer in
Romans 8 is entirely not a matter of faith but a matter of
praying with groanings in the Spirit. That groaning is in
death and resurrection. For example, a brother may have
offended you, criticized you, judged you, and attacked you, so
that you can no longer bear it. When you go before God to
pray, you intend to accuse him, but the Spirit will not allow
you to do so. Rather, He wants you to pray for that brother

and ask the Lord to be gracious to him. Many times you cannot pray thus, but you can only groan continually. This is the principle of death and resurrection.

Always keep this principle. When Korah and his company rebelled, Moses told them to take their censers and burn incense in them. According to the spiritual meaning, that burning of the incense exemplifies praying in the natural being and outside resurrection. Such prayer not only cannot bring in blessings, but will encounter God's judgment and bring in spiritual death. Hence, we must learn to offer prayers in resurrection that will be acceptable to God. Only such prayers will have authority and be of value. Now we understand the necessity for prayer to be in resurrection.

CHAPTER SEVENTEEN

ASCENSION AND PRAYER

I. THE ILLUSTRATION IN THE OLD TESTAMENT

In the Old Testament typology, both the Holy Place and the Holy of Holies denote the heavens, or the heavenly realm. The altar of offerings being in the outer court indicates that the cross is accomplished on the earth; whereas, the altar of incense being in the Holy Place indicates plainly that the standing of prayer must be in the heavenly realm. Prayer is not performed in the earthly sphere but in the heavenly sphere. Although we humans are on earth and seem to be praying on earth, every prayer that is acceptable to God should be uttered in the heavenly realm. The outer court is good for offering the sacrifices, not for burning the incense. The burning of incense is to be carried out in the Holy Place. The altar of incense is not positioned in the outer court, but in the Holy Place. This tells us that prayer must be in the heavenly realm.

II. THE POSITION OF ASCENSION

Resurrection is a life, whereas ascension is a position. Whenever we speak of resurrection, we need to know that it is a matter of life. Likewise, whenever we speak of ascension, we must understand that it is a matter of position. Ephesians 2 says that we the believers having been made alive together with Christ, were also raised, ascended, and seated together with Christ in the heavenlies. To be made alive means to obtain life, to be resurrected is to live in life, and to be ascended is to gain a heavenly standing. However, since we are clearly on earth, how can we be seated together in the heavenlies with Christ? We must know that, in the original Greek, "heavenlies" here does not refer to the physical heaven, but indicates a kind of heavenly state, heavenly atmosphere, and heavenly nature. Location-wise, of course, we are not yet in the heavenlies today; but according to state, atmosphere, and nature, we are definitely in the heavenlies. This is the meaning of the "heavenlies" spoken of in Ephesians 2. We have arrived at such a heavenly nature and heavenly state in the resurrected and ascended Christ. This is our position.

Let us give an illustration here. Suppose I visit a United States colony in the Philippines. Here the language, the food, the housing, the people, and everything they do are typical of the United States. Geographically speaking, I am in the Philippines, not the United States; but the atmosphere and nature make me feel that, without a doubt, I am in the United States. Thus, "heavenlies" in Ephesians 2 does not refer to a place but to a kind of atmosphere and nature. Of course, on the other hand, the "heavenlies" also denotes the place. Everyone who prays must see that ascension is a position, and that such a heavenly position means a heavenly atmosphere, a heavenly nature.

III. THE AUTHORITY OF ASCENSION

The position of ascension produces the authority of ascension. Anyone in any kind of position has the authority which corresponds to that position. Even a servant has the authority as well as the position of a servant. A policeman has the position and the authority of a policeman. A teacher has the position and the authority of a teacher. Therefore, we need to see that ascension is a position, and with such a position there is the corresponding authority. The spiritual life of a Christian is not only a matter of life, but also a matter of position. Hence, it is not only a matter of power but also a matter of authority. Life brings in power; while position brings in authority. Resurrection is a matter of power; whereas, ascension is a matter of authority. In order to have a certain measure or kind of authority you need to be in a certain position. If you are in the heavenly realm, you will spontaneously have the

heavenly authority. All our genuine prayers are the exercising of heavenly authority in the heavenly position.

IV. THE POSITION OF PRAYER

The position of prayer is the position of ascension. You can
only pray in the heavenly sphere. Whenever you leave the
heavenly realm, you lose the position of prayer. You may pray,
but that prayer does not count before God.

I can give you several simple but true examples. When I
was a boy I studied in a Christian school. That was during
World War I. I heard some smart ones asking the pastor,
"There are Christians in Germany, and there are also Christians in Great Britain, yet the two countries are implacable
enemies. We heard that the Christians in Germany are praying for the victory of Germany, and that the Christians in
Great Britain are praying for the victory of Great Britain.
Will you please tell us which side's prayer will be answered
by God?" Today, brothers and sisters, I would like to ask you
the same question. How would you answer? If I remember
correctly, the pastor answered wisely, saying, "God is not foolish, and being a righteous God, He will not foolishly answer
an unjust prayer." He did not say that God would answer the
prayers of the British or that God would answer the prayers
of the Germans. He simply gave an ambiguous answer and
dismissed the question.

Later, after I was saved, this question often came back
to me. Gradually I became clear about it. God would not
listen to the Christians in Germany, or Great Britain, as they
prayed on the position of their respective country. Neither
Great Britain nor Germany is the position of prayer. Whoever prays by standing either on the position of Great Britain
or Germany will never have his prayer answered by God.
There is only one position for prayer—that is the heavenly
position. You must pray in the heavenly sphere.

Let me give you another example. Suppose there is a
couple who always quarrel with one another. Both are saved
ones, yet their personalities are very incompatible. One
day the husband prays asking the Lord to deal with his
wife, and the wife also prays imploring the Lord to deal with

her husband. Whose prayer will God answer? Don't think that I am making up this story. It is a real case. A certain wife, wiping away her tears, prays to God, "O God, You are a just God. You are omniscient and know the wrongs that I have suffered. Do grant me justice." You hear the wife praying thus in one room, and going to another room, you hear the husband praying the same prayer from his viewpoint. Brothers and sisters, whose prayer will God answer? Neither! For they have fallen from heaven to earth. Since they have lost the position of prayer, God cannot answer their prayers.

Again, suppose two co-workers serve together yet cannot get along with each other. One of them prays, "Lord, this is really difficult for me. The condition of my brother is such that, unless You deal with him, I cannot take it any longer." The other one also prays, "Lord, this is really hard. Please come to intervene." Let me ask you, brothers and sisters, to which side will God attend? Please remember, there is no position of prayer here, for they do not pray in the heavens, but entirely on earth.

Some may even pray for the church in their locality or for the gospel there. These things are very good in themselves; but we still should ask, are they praying in the heavenly realm or on earth? There are a great number who pray for such things on earth, not in the heavenly sphere.

Some brothers may pray for their enterprise, and some sisters may pray for their husband's business, yet they pray on earth, not in the heavenly realm. Sometimes you notice that there are problems among the brothers and sisters, and you intend to pray for them. However, you realize that their problem has touched you and that you have been stirred up within before you go to pray. You are not in the heavenly realm, but on earth.

Hence, in prayer you need first to settle the matter of position. If you remain on earth you will have no way to pray, for the position of prayer is not on earth. Without the particular position, one cannot perform the particular task. Many times people ask, "Why didn't God answer our prayers?" Brothers and sisters, most likely it is because you have lost your standing of prayer. It may be that you still have a little anger or agitation causing you to argue for yourself and ask God to avenge and vindicate. This proves that you have left the heavenly sphere.

The New Testament says that God's children should only bless and not curse. Regardless how much people give you a hard time and persecute you, if you can still bless them, it proves that you are in the heavenly sphere. When Stephen was being martyred and stoned by men, he could still ask God to forgive them! His face resembled the face of an angel; he was in the sphere of the heavens. If one lives in the heavenly realm, he is able to love his enemies. Regardless how much trouble you give him, he can still love you. If a Christian hates his enemies and sounds out voices of cursing when being mistreated or persecuted, he is surely an earthly man.

Brothers and sisters, you may desire to pray for the church in your locality or for your evangelistic work. These are very good topics of prayer, but not having been dealt with, you still feel that the church and the work are "yours." You want "your" church here to prosper and increase in number that "your" work here may be fruitful. This also proves that you are not in the heavenly realm but have fallen to earth. If you wish to pray for these matters, you must first get into the heavenly position. Not only in these matters, but even when you get sick or encounter problems in your home and in your daily living, you must first get into the heavenly sphere when you are going to pray.

The position of prayer is entirely a heavenly position. You cannot have a bit of jealousy, spite, or anger toward others. Once these things are found in your prayers, immediately you are not in the heavenly realm. You are not burning the incense in the Holy Place. You may be burning incense on the street, being wholly on the earth and in the world. Hence, we have said that you may be able to do and say things freely at all times and on all occasions, except while in prayer. Prayer is not only a holy ground, but even more, it is a spiritual realm. The position of prayer is heavenly. Once you leave the heavenly sphere you lose the position of prayer.

V. THE AUTHORITY OF PRAYER

As the position of prayer is ascension, the authority of prayer is also ascension. With the position of prayer there is the authority of prayer. Whatever a Christian does is not only a matter of power, but even more, a matter of authority. For example, when preaching the Word you need not only power but also authority. This is true of some who pray before God. They not only have power but also authority, for they are in the heavenly position.

People often say that in prayer you need to remove sins, to have faith, and to hold on to God's promise. But gradually you will see that these do not always work. You may have been full of faith, yet God did not bring what you prayed for to pass. You held on to God's promise, yet the promise also failed. If you are willing to learn some lessons of prayer, you will gradually be able to see that it is not a matter of believing or holding on to the promise; rather, it is a matter of seeing the position of prayer through God's visitation. You will then be able to perform the task of prayer in the heavenly realm. At this time, your prayer is a prayer of authority. It is not a matter of your believing or holding on to the promise, but it is that you have the position and the authority to perform this task. God has no alternative but to approve such prayer, and He surely will approve it.

When you arrive at this place, you will know that there are certain things for which you cannot pray, because God does not allow you to do so. The most you can do is to discuss such a matter with God, saying, "O God, may I pray for this matter? If You will, please bring it to pass." You must not say, "O God, You must do this, for I have laid hold of Your promise." Why is it that at times when you pray in this way, no answer comes? It is because God has not given you that promise. This is not only a matter of dealing with sins or confessing your wrongs, but a matter of asking: where are you? what is your nature? and what kind of atmosphere are you in? If you are in the realm of the heavens, I am certain that eight out of ten of your prayers will be eliminated, for they are unnecessary, and you will not be able to pray them. You know that they are not the things for which you should pray in such a standing.

There is hardly anything else that demands from us more than prayer. Only in prayer can you see clearly what you are, what your condition is, and where you are. Generally, in other circumstances, you have no way to find out where you are, but once you are in prayer, you may discover that you are altogether outside the heavenly realm. For this reason, when one first believes in the Lord, he dares to pray for anything; but later, the longer he has been following the Lord, the narrower is the sphere of his prayers and the less bold he is in prayer. He dares not to pray for this and he dares not to pray for that. The more you grow in the Lord, the more you will realize that prayer has its position and sphere. In such a position and within such a sphere there can be such an authority.

VI. THE PRAYER OF AUTHORITY

All prayers in ascension are prayers of authority. We know that prayer in ascension is a command to God. Our prayer is not begging but commanding. You all remember that in Isaiah 45:11, God says, "Command ye me." Sometimes this commanding is a direct command to God, and sometimes it is an indirect command to the environment. Examples are: Moses standing on the shore of the Red Sea commanding the water to be divided, the Lord Jesus in the boat commanding the wind and the sea to be still, and the Lord commanding sickness to leave men. If you have learned to pray by standing in the realm of ascension, you can even command poverty to leave you. You are not there imploring, asking for God's mercy and visitation just like a beggar asking men for a little money. If you have touched the heavenly position with its authority, you can even say, "I command the poverty to depart from me." This is not our imagination. Some definitely have had such an experience.

In the Bible, on the one hand, it says that we should pray without ceasing, but on the other hand, it does not show us that answers to many prayers will be forthcoming according to what people expect. There have been occasions when brothers and sisters have come to me and immediately asked me to

pray for them. I really did not know how to pray for them, for
I did not know whether they were in heaven or on earth.
Brothers and sisters, anyone who can pray conveniently does
not know what prayer is. If you really know the position and
the authority of prayer, then you will know that worthwhile
prayer is not that easy.

Of course, God is gracious to us in all things, and He
always listens to our prayer. I admit this is true. However,
God also shows us that prayer is a matter of being in ascension. If you really wish to have some worthwhile prayers
before God, you need to be able to give out some authoritative
commands before God. Standing before God, I can tell you
that in the past years in some places, as we encountered some
problems in the work or in the church, we prayed this kind of
commanding prayer. We expressed ourselves boldly before
God, saying, "God, we cannot allow this matter." If your position is wrong and your condition is not in the heavenly realm,
such prayer would be an insult to God. But if your position is
right and your state is in the heavenly sphere, then such
prayer would be a real pleasure to Him. The words you pray
are equal to God's administration; they are equivalent to executing His commands. I can testify that God answers such
prayers.

It is not that when one goes out to the street and points
with a stick the cars will stop; rather, it is when the traffic
policeman points with his stick that everyone will stop, for he
has the position and the authority. The most simple and easy
prayers are these kind of commanding prayers, authoritative
prayers. But in order to have such prayers, you need to
acquire a position of ascension. What is a prayer of authority?
It is a prayer by one who is able to give out commands by
standing in the position of ascension.

Because our spiritual condition today is too low, very few
among the children of God know, and fewer actually practice
this kind of prayer. But if we go on properly in the Lord, we
will realize that we are in the Holy Place, not the outer court.
We will also realize that we are in the realm of ascension
and cannot be touched by numerous things. We are together
with the Lord in the realm of ascension and on the throne.

Therefore, we are able to give orders and command everything according to the Lord's will. Whatever we pray from such a position is an order, a command.

VII. THE PRAYER ON THE THRONE

When you come to the point where you have the heavenly position and the heavenly authority, and are thus able to utter forth authoritative prayers, you are one who is on the throne, standing in the ruling position together with the Lord. Just as He reigns at the right hand of God, so you also reign together with Him in the heavenly realm. At this time, your prayer is not only an authoritative prayer but also a reigning prayer. Your prayer is to rule with authority, executing God's orders. So at this time, all your prayers become God's administration, the execution of God's rule. Maybe I have gone too high, but I know that if we are willing to learn, we will arrive at a place where we can utter such prayers.

In summary, there is only one position for prayer—the heavenly sphere. Once you leave this sphere you lose the position of prayer. Prayer is not only concerned with certain matters; but, much more, it is concerned with a certain position. You need to be in the heavenly sphere. Then you have the position to pray, you are able to pray with authority, and you are one sitting on the throne, uttering forth prayers of the throne.

Chapter Eighteen

THE PRAYER OF WARFARE

In this chapter we will look at the matter of the prayer of warfare. If we have seen that the prayers of greatest worth are prayers in ascension, then we can easily understand that prayer is a warfare, and we will utter prayers of warfare. Such is the nature of the prayer spoken of in Ephesians 6. It is not the ordinary, common, general prayer. It is very high, being uttered from the realm of the heavens.

I. PRAYER AND THE KINGDOM OF GOD

God's kingdom is the sphere of God's rule. The Bible shows us that God's plan, on the positive side, is to have Himself expressed in His Son. On the negative side, God's plan is to have His authority carried out in the whole universe so that the entire universe may become His kingdom, the sphere of His rule. In reading the Scripture, we should always keep in mind the two aspects of God's plan.

From the outset, Genesis chapter one shows us God's image and God's dominion. God's intention in the universe is that He might be expressed and that His kingdom might not suffer any restriction. So the Lord Jesus began His prayer by saying, "Let Your name be sanctified" (Matt. 6:9), which is a matter of God being expressed. Then He said, "Let Your kingdom come; let Your will be done, as in heaven, so on earth" (Matt. 6:10). This is a matter of God's kingdom and God's dominion. The three "lets" in the Lord's prayer bespeak the two aspects of God's plan. Throughout the centuries, almost all who are in Christianity have paid much attention to the Lord's prayer. Every day there are people who recite it; but, unfortunately, the words of this prayer seem to be closed to them. May the Lord grant us mercy and show us that His prayer is for the unlimited spread of the kingdom of God on the earth and in the whole universe. Of course, in order to carry out such a plan of God, there is the need for God's people to pray sufficiently. The true prayers of God's people are for His kingdom. You and I may pray for numerous things, but unless the ultimate purpose is for God's kingdom, those prayers are of no value before God. We admit that in the Lord's prayer there is the matter of dealing with sins and the matter of the daily living, but its beginning and ending are entirely for the kingdom of God. In the beginning it says, "Let Your kingdom come; let Your will be done on earth." At the end it says, "For Yours is the kingdom, and the power, and the glory forever." Therefore, this prayer shows us that He wants our prayer to be wholly for God's kingdom.

The situation in Revelation 12 depicts the true prayers of the saints. There we are shown the woman bringing forth a man-child. The woman signifies the totality of the redeemed ones. The man-child signifies the stronger part of the redeemed people, that is, the overcomers in the church. We need to realize that the woman and the man-child whom she brought forth did pray. Their voices reached God, so following the rapture of the man-child there was war in heaven. Consequently, God's enemy was cast out from heaven to the earth. Then there was a loud voice in heaven saying, "Now is come the salvation and the power and the kingdom of our God and the authority of His Christ" (Rev. 12:10). Hence, once God's people utter the real prayers, the result is always the ushering in of God's kingdom. On the other hand, without the prayers of God's people, there is no way for God's kingdom to come. The coming of the kingdom is absolutely related to our prayers.

The examples in the Old Testament also confirm this. When the children of Israel were in captivity, Jerusalem was destroyed, the temple was burnt, and the nation of Israel was in complete collapse. At that time God raised up several men of prayer in Babylon. Daniel and three of his friends were competent in prayer. Their prayers brought in the kingdom. God's kingdom had come to the earth through David, but after Solomon's time it was defeated again. In Babylon, Daniel was praying precisely for this matter, so that God's kingdom might be brought back once more to the earth. It was completely due to Daniel's prayer that God was able to build the temple, restore Jerusalem, and have the dominion. Therefore, we must be clear that whether or not God's kingdom can come and whether or not He can rule on earth all depend on whether or not God's people will pray. The ultimate purpose of prayer is for bringing in God's kingdom.

II. PRAYER AND GOD'S ENEMY

Prayer is categorically related to God's enemy. God's authority is under attack in the universe because of the existence of God's enemy. In the Bible, the kingdom of God is of great significance. The enemy of God is also a very crucial issue in the Scripture. God's authority suffers frustration and limitation in the universe because there is a rebellious Satan in the universe.

There is a very great conflict in the universe between God and His enemy Satan. You may say that the Bible is a book of life, and you may also say that the Bible is a book of warfare. There is a line in the Scripture which is the line of warfare. Satan firstly rose to revolt and to rebel. Then God came out to deal with him, and the universal warfare began. Today's worldly statesmen and military experts are searching for ways to eliminate war and promote peace. They do not understand that the happenings on the earth are entirely tied to the warfare between God and Satan. When will peace come to the human race? That will have to wait until the day when God's enemy shall be bound and cast into the bottomless pit. Then in the whole universe there will be no more war between God and Satan, and likewise, wars among the human race will cease. Human warfare stems entirely from the universal warfare between God and the Devil. When the universal warfare is settled there will be no more wars among men. Hence, we should utter prayers of warfare, on one hand, to bring in God's kingdom and, on the other hand, to drive out God's enemy. Prayer indicates that man is standing on God's side and that man is opposed to God's enemy.

There are three main figures in the universe: God, Satan, and man. Never belittle man. God has never belittled man. God, Satan, and man may be considered the three big heads in the universe. Satan's intention is to overthrow God's authority. God's desire is to do away with the rebellious Satan. However, God does not wish to deal with Satan directly, and Satan has no way to destroy God's authority by his own strength. God needs to work through man to deal with Satan, and Satan also needs to work through man to frustrate God. The solution to the problems existing between God and the Devil are tied to man. Man is the critical figure in the universe. If man stands on God's side, God predominates. If man stands on Satan's side, then Satan prevails.

There is a line of truth in the Bible which is concerned with the conflict between God and Satan. This line necessarily includes God and Satan's struggle to gain man. God wants to have man, and Satan also wants to gain man. God wants man to cooperate with Him; Satan also wants man to cooperate with him. God wants to enter into man; Satan also wants to get into man. God wants to be mingled with man; Satan also wants to be mixed with man. In this context, what is prayer? On the one hand, prayer is man expressing to God that he wants God and that he is standing on God's side. On the other hand, it is man telling Satan that he is standing with God to oppose Satan. Hence, the purpose of prayer is to bring in God's kingdom and to drive Satan away.

Our ordinary concept in praying for sinners is to pray that their soul would be saved. But the fact is, true prayers for men's souls are to deal with Satan and to bring in God's kingdom. When a person does not believe in the Lord Jesus, it is not just a matter of his soul going to hell. Even more, it is a matter of Satan's ruling over him. His going to hell is a matter bound up with the great matter of Satan's ruling over him. So, I need to pray for him in order to chase Satan away from him, to deliver him from the power of darkness, and to bring God's kingdom to him. True prayers will always, on the one hand, bring God's kingdom to man and, on the other hand, drive away Satan's power from man. Every time a sinner gets saved it signifies a partial defeat of Satan's power and a partial coming of God's kingdom. This is the prayer of warfare.

In the Bible it is a very great principle that God Himself does not deal with Satan directly. Rather, He uses man. Some may say: "Isn't God dealing with Satan through His Son? The Scripture says, 'For this purpose the Son of God was manifested, that he might destroy the works of the devil'" (1 John 3:8). Yes, this is true. But the Son of God came to deal with Satan in the human flesh. He came as a man standing on man's position and put on man to deal with Satan. To deal with His enemy, God needs to use man. If man does not cooperate with Him, He cannot do anything. Likewise, to bring salvation to man, God also needs man to pray. Without man praying for the souls of sinners, God can never save men. The salvation of any person is the result of someone praying for him. God has no way to save men directly. God's salvation is indirect; it needs to go through man. Here we see how crucial man's position is. Man's prayer indicates whether he is standing on God's side or on Satan's. Once you bow your knees before God, you indicate that in the universal conflict you are standing on God's side, and you are totally opposed to God's enemy. Your prayer is, positively, bringing in God's kingdom and, negatively, overthrowing God's enemy.

Every genuine prayer is a prayer of casting out the demons. Suppose a certain brother's home has no peace. The husband and wife quarrel. If you really know what prayer is, you will be able to utter fighting prayers for them and cast out the quarreling demon from their home. I really mean it. The husband and wife quarrel because Satan has gained a position between them. When you pray for them, on the one hand, you are bringing in God's kingdom and, on the other hand, driving away God's enemy. Then between them there will be God's authority but no power of Satan. This is true prayer.

This is also true concerning prayer for the church. Disagreements and contentions are in the church because Satan has gained a place. So we pray for the church in order to bring in God's kingdom and drive out Satan's power. All genuine prayers are of a two-fold purpose: on the positive side, to bring in God's kingdom, and on the negative side, to cast out Satan's power. This kind of prayer effects God's success as well as Satan's defeat. The more we pray this kind of prayer, the more severe will be Satan's defeat, and the more God's kingdom will come.

III. THE POSITION OF GOD'S ENEMY

We shall now look at the position of God's enemy. Speaking of the spiritual warfare, Ephesians 6 tells us that God's enemy, the power of darkness, is in the air. Both in Ephesians and Colossians there are several places which tell us that the rulers and the authorities are in the air. So the position of God's enemy is in the air. On the other hand, the Bible also shows us that the sphere of the activities of God's enemy is on earth. Satan usurps the air as his dwelling place and controls the earth as the sphere of his activities. So the Lord Jesus wants us to pray that God's kingdom may come and that God's will may be done on earth as it is in heaven. The whole earth today, on the one hand, is under God's rule. But on the other hand, if you observe the situation everywhere, you will sense that no one cares for God's will and God's authority, for the whole earth has been usurped by Satan.

If you can visualize the situation, you will see that God is in the heavens, Satan is in the air, and man is on the earth. The entire earth is under the control of the air, and man is under the control of Satan. Daniel chapter ten reveals that as Daniel prayed earnestly and set his heart to understand, God sent a messenger from the heavens telling him that his prayers were heard. The angel encountered the prince of Persia in the air and was not able to get through. The fighting lasted three weeks. Eventually Michael came to help the angel, who was then able to get through the air and come to Daniel on the earth. Such passages in the Bible make known to us the spiritual things in the universe. Satan usurps the air and controls the earth. If Hades, which is underneath the earth, is added, then three out of the four places in the universe are held in Satan's hands. Only the heaven is left for God. Such is the position of Satan.

IV. THE POSITION OF PRAYER

The position of prayer is the position of ascension. All who do not pray from the position of ascension fall under the control of Satan. Genuine prayers are always uttered in the heavenly realm. Mrs. Penn-Lewis once said that one must first see clearly the position of ascension in Ephesians 2 in order to have the fighting prayers in Ephesians 6. Once you fall to the earth you are under Satan's hand, and you will not be able to deal with him. Daniel's prayer was, on the one hand, on earth, and on the other hand, in the heavenly realm. His condition and nature were entirely heavenly, so his prayer was able to deal with the enemy.

Take the example of a family where both the husband and the wife are saved ones. One day, however, the husband and wife quarrel with one another. Being unable to settle the dispute between themselves, both come to the responsible brothers to present their accusations. The husband says how much the sister is giving him a difficult time, and the wife says how much the brother wrongs her. Upon hearing the case, some immediately say, "This sister is unreasonable! She is altogether out of line. She doesn't have her head covered, nor does she stand in her position." But some who stand on the sister's side say, "That brother is unreasonable. How can he be so unsympathetic and inconsiderate?" May I ask you, when a brother and sister quarrel in this way, are they in the heavens, on the earth, or in the air? I believe we all know that by quarreling everyone invariably tumbles down from heaven. Maybe a week ago we were praising God, saying, "We have been seated together with Christ in the heavenlies, Hallelujah!" But before we have sung Hallelujah for very long, we all tumble down from heaven. We all are on the earth. And not only so, even those who have heard this brother and sister's case also become involved and fall from the ascended position. Some fall to the earth together with the sister, and others fall with the brother. Those in defense of the sister and those in defense of the brother all come to pray. Those who take the side of the sister go before God saying, "Lord, see how unbecoming that brother is. We cannot imagine that one

who serves You can be such." And those who take the side of
the brother also pray, saying, "Lord, what shall we do? If even
such a sister who serves You behaves like this, henceforth,
how can the church help the sisters?" Let me ask you, what
are these prayers? If you would allow me such an expression,
I would say that this is a prayer of rolling on the ground. It is
a prayer of the blood and of the flesh. Blood and flesh are
earthly, so these are prayers of the earth.

You must be an ascended one in order to pray for others. If
you are stirred by a particular matter and act in your flesh,
you fall from the heaven to the earth and cannot pray. You
cannot pray for those things until the Lord shows His mercy,
and you recover your ascended position. One who is unable to
pray surely is on the earth. When others quarrel and you
become involved in it, you lose your position to pray. Under
such circumstances, you have no way to deal with God's
enemy.

After reading Daniel's prayer, you must admit that he was
really one who had ascended to the heavens, entered the
Holy of Holies, and touched the throne. Although he was one
who lived on earth, he lived in the realm of the heavenlies.
Therefore, his prayer was powerful, being able to solve the
problems of God's people on the earth.

This is the principle of prayer, not only when we pray for
big things such as God's will and God's work, but even when
we pray for ourselves—our health, our family, and our business. Always keep in mind that Satan's position is in the air.
Therefore, if we pray on the earth, we will be under his control. But if we move to the heavens and pray, we pray down
from above. In military strategy, this is to observe and control
the situation below by occupying the high ground. This is
exactly like the prayers in Revelation 8. As far as fragrance is
concerned, the prayers ascended to God; but as far as God's
accomplishment is concerned, the prayers were prayed down
from heaven. They were poured down from heaven, because
they were all uttered in the heavenly realm. Concerning
God's acceptance, our prayers should be like sweet-smelling
incense ascending to the throne; but with regard to the dealing with the enemy, our prayers should be poured down from

the throne. All true men of prayer are seated together with Christ in the heavenlies and pray from the throne.

V. PRAYER ON THE THRONE

A prayer such as that just referred to is a prayer on the throne, even a reigning prayer. Man's emotion, temper, flesh, opinion, and grievance need to be thoroughly dealt with in such a case. Whenever we have a grievance or anger, we fall from the heavens to the earth and immediately lose our position of ascension to pray. Thus, we have no way to pray.

VI. PRAYER OF WARFARE

All prayers that are expressed in the heavenly realm and from the throne of God are prayers of warfare. He who prays in this way is one who has passed through the cross, resurrected, and ascended. He is on the throne, far above the earth, and is not touched by any earthly thing. The prayers which he expresses from such a realm are prayers that can defeat the Devil in the air and bring down God's authority. Like Daniel's prayer, such prayer is able to bring the things of heaven to the earth. It is able to get the heavenly authority through the air and bring it to the earth. This is the fighting prayer.

Please consider: is there a sinner who does not want to be saved? Is there a saint who does not want to love the Lord? All sinners want to be saved, and all saints desire to love the Lord. But because there is someone in the air who usurps men and controls the men on earth, sinners are prevented from receiving the gospel, and saints are hindered from seeking the Lord. So it is not enough that we only preach the gospel and minister the Word. We must rise up and live in the heavenly realm to touch the throne of God as Daniel did. We must pray to God that God's heavenly authority may be brought down to the earth. If this is done, you will see that one by one sinners will be saved, and one by one saints will rise up to seek and love the Lord. For here there are fighting prayers driving away the power of darkness, bringing in God's authority, and as a result, causing God to have His will done on earth. They enable God to carry out His salvation and give grace to His children according to His good pleasure.

So every praying person should be one who is in the heavenly realm, touching God's throne, and therefore, able to pour down prayers from heaven. As you are above the earth, the air, and the power of darkness, and are seated together with Christ on the throne of God in the heavenlies, the prayers you utter are prayers of warfare. Having understood this point, you will turn the focus of your attention from man to the Devil. When a sinner fails to receive salvation, you should pray, "O God, it is not that he would not repent, but it is the Devil that is usurping him. I pray that You cast out the Devil from him." When the husband and the wife are in a family quarrel, you will not blame the brother or the sister. Your eyes will see that the brother and the sister are under the power of darkness. So the target of your prayers will not be the brother or sister, but the power of darkness that is behind them and on them. This is the wrestling spoken of in Ephesians 6. This is not wrestling against blood and flesh, but against the spiritual forces of evil in the heavenlies. The target with which we are dealing in our prayers is not man but the Devil. All the problems in the church are not with the brothers and sisters, but with Satan. The problems in the family also are not with the husband, the wife, or the children, but with Satan. The object of the prayer of spiritual warfare is not at all men of blood and flesh, but the Devil of the spiritual realm. If we are in the heavenly realm, we are able to pray such prayers of ascension, that is, prayers of warfare. Such prayers of warfare are for the driving out of Satan and the ushering in of God's kingdom.

Chapter Nineteen

FASTING AND PRAYER

Christians are very familiar with the matter of fasting in prayer, but unfortunately, many misunderstand its meaning and treat it as a common thing. I am afraid that there are not many who really know what it means to fast and pray. Now let us come to the Bible and take a good look into this matter.

When the Bible first mentions prayer, it does not speak of the need to fast. You do not see either Noah or Abraham praying with fasting. The case of Moses is somewhat different. The Bible does not explicitly say that he fasted and prayed, but it seems certain that he did when he went up to God on Mount Sinai. From that time onward, the Bible frequently mentions the matter of fasting in prayer. Especially in the New Testament, it is very evident that fasting is greatly related to prayer. The first man who fasted in the New Testament was John the Baptist. Matthew 11:18 says "John came neither eating nor drinking." Of course, that does not mean that John fasted absolutely. It means that he took no part in the worldly enjoyment. On the one hand, John neither ate nor drank, and on the other hand he still ate "locusts and wild honey" (Matt. 3:4). In any case, he should be listed among those who fasted.

In the New Testament record, the second person who fasted was the Lord Jesus. When the Lord first came forth to minister, He fasted before God for forty days. Later, in His teaching, He also spoke something about fasting. He said that while He was with the disciples they did not need to fast, but when He would be taken away from them, they would have to fast (Mark 2:18-20). He also said that some demons cannot be cast out by prayer alone (Matt. 17:21). So by the example of the Lord Jesus, we can see that He was a real fasting One. At the same time, His teachings show us what fasting actually is. Later on, the Bible shows us that during the apostolic age, the apostles often fasted and prayed. Acts 13 gives a very clear record of five prophets and teachers in the church at Antioch who fasted and prayed while they ministered to the Lord. In particular, when two among them were to be sent to the Gentiles, they fasted and prayed before sending them away. We may say that the record of fasting reaches its climax in Acts 13.

I have very briefly pointed out the relationship between fasting and prayer. From these records we can actually see what the relationship is between fasting and prayer, or what is the meaning of fasting in prayer.

I. FASTING IS THE SPONTANEOUS EXPRESSION OF MAN RECEIVING GREAT RESPONSIBILITY

First, fasting is a spontaneous expression as man receives a great responsibility before God. At such a time, man will spontaneously fast. The experiences in our human life also substantiate this point. Often when we encounter an important matter in the course of our human living, we become unable to eat. True, some matters can make us happy and cause us to eat more, but other matters may press us to a point that we simply cannot eat. Because the matter which we encounter is so great and the responsibility so heavy, we spontaneously lose our appetite for food. However, when the matter is taken care of and the responsibility discharged, we feel relieved and our appetite returns for normal eating. Likewise, as we receive a great matter from God, we are so burdened within that we fast without purposing to do so. Because Moses received a great responsibility from God on Mount Sinai, he was unable to eat for forty days. Later on, as the Lord Jesus came forth to minister, having received great responsibility, he was also unable to eat. This does not mean that He actually could not eat. It means that He had no heart to eat. It was as if there were no room in Him to contain food. In Acts 13, a tremendous responsibility was placed upon the prophets and teachers in Antioch. Therefore, they spontaneously fasted and prayed in order to spare their whole being any distraction from that responsibility. This is the first meaning of fasting.

II. FASTING IS AN INDICATION OF MAN'S ABSOLUTENESS

Second, fasting is man's indication that he stands absolutely on God's side. In the chapter concerning the prayer of warfare we said that prayer is man declaring in the universe that he is standing on God's side to oppose Satan. Fasting is a sign of the absoluteness of such prayer. Today, in order to show his absoluteness concerning a certain matter, a man may fast a long time. If you can be praying for a certain matter and can also be eating, it reveals that you are not absolutely standing on God's side. It demonstrates that your attitude is still not firm enough. So, brothers and sisters, as you pray, do not fast lightly. Always keep in mind that in fasting you are saying, "Here is a great and important matter, and in this matter, my attitude, my intention, is one hundred percent, absolutely standing on God's side to oppose God's enemy."

III. FASTING IS THE RENUNCIATION OF LAWFUL RIGHT

Third, the basic meaning of fasting is to renounce one's lawful rights. There is nothing in our human life that is more legitimate than eating. Following the creation of man, the first thing God did for man was to arrange the matter of eating. In Genesis 1, after He created man according to His image, God immediately ordained the herbs and fruits as food for man. Therefore, man's eating is lawful. By his fasting, man indicates that in order to receive and bear an important matter he renounces his most legitimate right.

Since fasting is the renunciation of our lawful right, we also must learn to give up our legitimate rights in many other matters. If we are not willing to put aside the enjoyments of our life as we fast, then such fasting is meaningless. The Lord Jesus' life matched His fasting, because while living as a man on the earth, He gave up many lawful rights. The entire life of the Lord Jesus was based on the principle of fasting. He

renounced His lawful rights and forsook His reasonable
enjoyments, so that although He did not fast daily, He lived
every day in the principle of fasting.

IV. FASTING IS MAN INDICATING
THAT HE DOES NOT CARE FOR HIMSELF

Fourth, fasting also indicates that man does not care for
himself, not even for his life. Eating is most crucial to human
existence. Without eating, man will starve to death. Hence, to
fast is to use your life as a pledge. In fasting you are saying, "I
want this matter to be fulfilled even at the cost of my life.
I am fighting for it with my life." Sometimes people working
in an organization may argue about something and use their
staying or leaving as a pledge. In essence, they say, "If you
agree with me, I will stay; if not, I will leave." Keep in mind
that fasting is fighting for something with your life. You are,
in effect, maintaining the attitude that you would rather die
than let this matter pass by. You would die in order that this
matter might be carried out. Thus, if we pray for a certain
burden, and within our heart we still consider our future, our
destiny, or our life, then we may pray, but we do not need to
fast. If you really want to fast and pray for a certain matter,
you need to maintain the attitude that you are putting your
life aside. This is in accordance with what the apostle Paul
said, "Neither count I my life as dear unto myself" (Acts
20:24). When Paul was on his way to Jerusalem for the last
time, all along the way believers warned him, saying, "When
you get there, you will surely be bound with chains and
encounter danger." They besought him to such an extent that
Paul, being unable to bear it, answered, "What mean ye to
weep and to break mine heart? for I am ready not to be bound
only, but also to die at Jerusalem for the name of the Lord
Jesus" (Acts 21:13). This is the principle of fasting. In fasting,
you not only renounce your rights, but you also give up your
life. Therefore, when we sometimes feel that our fasting is
meaningless, it is because we are merely manifesting an outward indication, while inwardly we are still the same. Fasting
means that a certain matter is pressing upon you to such an
extent that you have to fight with your life and that you

would rather die than allow this matter to go by lightly. You will prove this matter to God even unto death. When you have such a strong feeling, your fasting is meaningful.

V. FASTING IS FOR THE ACCOMPLISHMENT OF GOD'S WILL AND FOR THE DEFEAT OF SATAN

Fifth, fasting is for God's will to be accomplished and for Satan to be defeated. The instances of fasting and prayer that are recorded in the Bible are either for the accomplishment of God's will or for the driving out of the Devil. It is difficult to find even one example that is for man's own benefit. Hence, we may conclude that real fasting is, on one hand, to accomplish God's will and, on the other hand, to get rid of Satan. Perhaps you will ask, "When we fast and pray for the healing of our sickness, can we say that this is also for God's will to be accomplished and for Satan to be removed?" The issue is this: if your concept and viewpoint are purely for God's healing then your fasting is useless. You need to receive mercy, become enlightened, and be led to such an extent that even though your sickness may be so serious that there is no hope for recovery, you will still say to God, "O God, if You keep me on this earth, all my days henceforth shall be absolutely for You; if not, may You allow me to die quickly. I don't want to live for myself on this earth. O God, I am asking You to do one thing here today, that I may be healed and that I may live henceforth wholly for You." If you have such a condition, such a heart, and such a thought, you are already fasting. I believe that most sickness will be healed at such a point.

Allow me to add a few words here concerning healing. Never believe that divine healing is absolutely unconditional and unlimited. As far as God's power is concerned, it is indeed unlimited, but as far as men who receive the divine healing are concerned, there is still a limit. Brothers and sisters, I would like to tell you that those who have received divine healing in the past have eventually still died. Even Lazarus, after having been raised from death, eventually died. We have to wait until the coming day of resurrection to receive the unlimited divine healing. Today there is no sickness that is absolutely and completely healed. Tens of thousands in the church have received divine healing in the last two thousand years, but where are they today? They are all in tombs; they are in death waiting for the ultimate healing. Hence, Brother Darby wrote: "Waiting for Him who takes us up beyond the power of death" (*Hymns,* #47). Although you and I have not entered into tombs, we are in death. All sicknesses are factors of death. Actually, before resurrection comes, everyone who is healed receives but a temporary healing. Today, in times of necessity, God gives us limited healing. He allows us to live a few more years on this earth, but it is not for our health or for our longevity, but for His will.

Brothers, this does not mean, therefore, that when you are sick and you fast and pray, God will necessarily heal you. What fasting means is that you are here absolutely for God's will to be done and for God's enemy to be cast out. As to whether or not you will be healed, that is another matter. Having realized that you were altogether living for yourself in the past, you repent to God and ask Him that, if it pleases Him, He keep you on this earth for another period of time. You tell Him that you desire to have His will fully accomplished in you and to give Satan no ground whatsoever in you. I repeat, however, this healing is temporary. It is so that His will may be accomplished in you. Otherwise, no matter how you fast and pray, it is still futile. Never think that as long as you fast and pray, your prayer will be answered by God. The basic principle of fasting in prayer is to indicate that you absolutely care for God's will to be accomplished and for Satan to be removed. You cannot find an illustration in the Bible showing that when man fasts and prays for his personal interest God answers that prayer. Never imagine that if your business is losing money, and your whole family fasts and prays, tomorrow your business will prosper. This is absolutely not the case. This is superstition. Fasting in prayer in the Bible is always this: either man on earth has touched God's desire and asks God to fulfill it, or he has encountered God's enemy and desires to cast him out.

VI. DO NOT FAST LIGHTLY

Since the meaning of fasting is so serious, I would advise

you, brothers and sisters, not to fast lightly. We cannot find in the Gospels that the Lord Jesus frequently fasted. Never consider fasting a trifling matter. Only the hypocritical Pharisees would say that they fasted twice a week. They considered fasting very common. In the Old Testament, the prophet Isaiah severely rebuked such fasting. God does not accept such fasting in prayer. Do not regard fasting as a religious form, nor treat it as a superstitious requirement. The fasting in prayer which God accepts occurs when one receives a commission from God which is very great. Because he loves God and cares so much for His purpose, he is willing to give up his right to legitimate enjoyment. He also is willing to struggle for that commission to the death. In that instance, such a person would spontaneously fast.

VII. FASTING IS NECESSARY

On the one hand, a Christian should not fast lightly, but on the other hand, he needs to fast. If a Christian has never fasted, there is certainly something wrong with him. Either God has never committed any matter to him, or he has refused God's commission. If you have never sensed that there is a great responsibility coming from God to you, it simply means that you have never indicated to God with a firm attitude that you want His will and want to stand on His side. You regard the things of God as unimportant. Whether the gospel is preached or not, and whether or not sinners are saved are of no consequence to you. After all, you have already prayed for them. So after your prayer, you are still able to eat and drink in merriment. Brothers and sisters, if such is your attitude, you are indeed a poor Christian! You do not care at all whether or not the church is in desolation. You care never to miss a meal. Since you do not have the life-and-death attitude toward the things of God, this proves that your Christian life is very lacking. If you would care a little for God's heart, the burden for the gospel would press upon you, and you would struggle in life and death. You would pray, "O God, the gospel must be powerful. You must save some, otherwise I can't eat or drink." This is what it means to fast and pray. You may also be so concerned for the House of God that you can say to God, "O God, it is all right for me to die, but it is not all right for the church to be in such a desolate state. Unless You solve the problem of the desolation of the church, I would rather die." I can tell you, brothers and sisters, at this point you will surely fast. It is an awful thing if God's children have never had such an experience, for it proves that they do not care for God's purpose or sense how fierce God's enemy is. So, what does fasting mean? Fasting means that you care very much for God's purpose, and you deeply sense the fierceness of God's enemy. Such sensation presses and compels you to such an extent that you simply cannot eat, drink, and be merry like other men, but that you must fast.

VIII. THE TEST FOR FASTING

Now we come to the test for fasting. How do you know that you need to fast? This is determined by whether or not you feel hungry when you do not eat. If when you do not eat you feel hungry and desire food, it proves you should not have fasted. If you do not feel hungry when you do not eat or thirsty when you do not drink, then you ought to fast. Sometimes the brothers and sisters would say, "Let us all fast!" But having fasted only that morning, at eleven o'clock someone may say, "Oh, I am really hungry." Let me tell you, your fasting that morning was wrong, and you should not have done it. All who truly fast will not feel hungry. Suppose one day a sister who is a widow should lose her only son. Undoubtedly, she could go without eating for three days without feeling hungry. Others might be concerned for her, and say, "Sister, you have not eaten for three days. How can this be?" She would say, "I am not hungry at all. I simply cannot take food."

Therefore, while fasting, if the brothers and sisters feel hungry, it is better for them to go quickly and get something to eat than to be hypocritical and sin against God. You should fast because you are so fully occupied with the problem and burden that at that moment you have no appetite and feel there is no room in you for food. Therefore, whether you should fast depends on whether you feel hungry. If you feel hungry, then do not fast; otherwise, fast.

IX. A FEW THINGS TO TAKE HEED OF

Finally, let us look at a few things that we must heed in the matter of fasting and prayer. First, if a burden truly presses you to such an extent that you cannot help but fast, then remember this: never fast without praying. You must fast *and* pray. Try your best to turn your fasting time, your fasting attitude, and your burden in fasting into prayer. All the experienced ones know that this kind of fasting in prayer is altogether outside any kind of form. It does not require thinking or memorizing, but issues entirely from within. Fasting without prayer is a great loss. Your body will suffer harm, your mind will be damaged, and even your spirit will suffer loss. Furthermore, without prayer, it is also hard for your burden to be carried out. Therefore, whenever you have a heavy burden that presses you to the extent that you cannot help but fast, you must do your best to pray. Such prayer will become food to your spirit. It affords you a considerable amount of mental comfort and will supply strength to your body. Fasting without prayer consumes you, but fasting with prayer supplies you.

Next, while you fast in prayer, always beware of having too many things as your burden. Do not pray for things apart from your burden. You do well just to pray specifically for that one matter. Why are you so heavy laden? Why can you not eat? Why are you not hungry? You should pray specifically for that one matter. It may be for the gospel; it may be for the church, or it may be for someone's soul to be saved. Our mistake is that while fasting, we still have our mind on many other things. If you come to the Lord with so many things to pray for, then you should not fast, because you have not reached the point where you can neither eat nor drink but can only pray before God.

Real fasting in prayer is this: because a person loves God, lives before God, and touches God's heart, the Spirit of God will heavily burden him with one thing that God desires to do. He will become burdened to such an extent that he can neither eat nor drink. Then he will spontaneously fast and go before God to pray. Consequently, such prayer will accomplish

God's purpose, drive out the Devil, and usher in God's authority.

Lastly, you need to take heed that when you really have
the burden to fast, you do not overdo it. Learn to be balanced
before God. Never think this way: "Did not the Lord Jesus fast
for forty days? Did not Moses also spend forty days on the
mountain? So it does not matter if I fast for eight or ten days."
Over twenty years ago I saw a sister who fasted too much. As
a result, her body became extremely weak and her mind
became very weary. Satan thus took the opportunity to attack
her. No one was able to help her. Eventually she fasted unto
death. Therefore, on one hand, we should not fast lightly, but
on the other hand, we should not overdo it. Rather, we should
stop at a certain point and thus be balanced.

Finally, I hope that among us, at every place and every
moment, there are some who are praying with fasting. During
the course of our service to the Lord, we should always come
to a point where we are unable to get through some matters,
and at that time we must fast and pray to deal with them.

CHAPTER TWENTY

IN THE LORD'S NAME AND PRAYER

Let us read several verses from the Gospel of John. "And whatever you ask in My Name, that will I do, that the Father may be glorified in the Son" (John 14:13).

"You did not choose Me, but I chose you, and I appointed you that you should go forth and bear fruit, and that your fruit should remain; that whatever you ask the Father in My name, He may give you" (John 15:16).

"Until now you have asked nothing in My name; ask, and you shall receive, that your joy may be made full. In that day you shall ask in My name..." (John 16:24, 26).

There are a great number of Christians who do not know that it is necessary to pray in the name of the Lord. Many Christians often say that they pray by the precious blood of the Lord or by the Lord's merits. The Bible clearly states, however, that we should pray *in the name of the Lord*. What does praying in the Lord's name really mean? Although we often use such a phrase, we do not necessarily know its meaning. Although some may know a little about it, they may not necessarily have the reality of it. The spiritual meaning of praying in the Lord's name is very deep and high, so we really need to go before the Lord to learn about it.

I. THE MEANING OF "IN THE NAME OF THE LORD"

In the Gospel of John, chapters fourteen through sixteen, the Lord Jesus personally says at least five times that we need to pray in His name. In Ephesians 5:20 the apostle Paul also says, "Giving thanks at all times for all things in the name of our Lord Jesus Christ to God and the Father." In John, chapters fourteen through sixteen, we should know

that the Lord's name undoubtedly denotes the Son. The name
of the Father in the same chapters also denotes the Father.
Hence, if we want to know the meaning of the Lord's name in
the Gospel of John, we need to know something concerning
the matter of the Lord coming to be the Son. What is the
meaning of "the Son"? We have said many times that the Son
is the expression of the Father. God has a Son in the universe,
and this Son is the expression of God. Whenever John chapters fourteen through sixteen mention the Lord Jesus, the
emphasis is not that He is the Lord nor that He is the Christ,
but that He is the Son. As the Son, He is the expression of
God. This name, therefore, is God's expression. To be in such a
name is to be in the expression of God.

We must see that in John 14 through 16 there is a
basic concept concerning a threefold matter: the Father is
expressed in the Son; the Son becomes the Spirit and enters
into us, and as a result, the Spirit lives out a certain life in us.
The Triune God—Father, Son, and Spirit—thus becomes one
with us. This is what John chapters fourteen through sixteen
disclose to us. Immediately following, in chapter seventeen,
the Lord offered a prayer in which He clearly shows us how
the Triune God—Father, Son, and Spirit—and we become
perfectly one.

In the Gospel of John there are three main concepts. The
first concept is that the Father has been expressed in the Son.
The Father has been seen and touched in the Son by men.
John 14:9 says that he who has seen the Son has seen the
Father. When the Son is in the midst of men, it is the Father
Who is in the midst of men. The second concept is that the
Son had to go and change His form to become the Spirit. The
third concept is that the Spirit comes into us who belong to
Him, to be with us forever. Consequently, as He lives, we also
live. We live together with Him, and we live by Him.

So, in chapter fifteen, we are shown just such a union. The
Lord says that He is the true Vine and we are the branches.
We abide in Him and He abides in us. Then, in chapter six-
teen, the Lord shows us how the Spirit reveals all His reality
into us so that we may experience and be led into the reality.
Therefore, in these chapters of John the Lord tells us that we

need to pray while living on the earth, and we need to pray in His name.

Based on the above-mentioned concepts, we know that praying in the Lord's name bespeaks the fact that we have a perfect union with the Lord, and that such a union causes God to be manifested in us. We need three chapters of the Scripture, John 14 through 16, to explain the matter of praying in the Lord's name. When we have a thorough understanding of these three chapters, we know what it means to pray in the Lord's name. Briefly, it means that we are in union with the Lord. The Lord is the expression of God; this expression has become the Spirit, and the Spirit is dwelling in us. When we have this perfect union with the Triune God, our living becomes His living, and God is manifested through us.

Please remember, therefore, that to pray in the name of the Lord means that we are united with the Lord, and we allow God to be manifested through us. Never consider "in the name of the Lord" as a phrase or a form that you have to use at the end of every prayer. At times it may not be necessary to add "in the name of the Lord" at the end of a prayer. To add "in the name of the Lord" does not necessarily mean there is the reality, and not adding it does not mean that the reality of it is missing. It is not a matter of formality, but a matter of reality. A person who really prays in the name of the Lord is one with the Lord. His prayer, therefore, is the Lord's asking. He has been united with the Lord to such an extent that the two have become one.

Never understand praying in the name of the Lord in a superstitious way. More than once I have heard people explain it by using the following illustration: you have asked a rich man for something, but he would not give it to you. Later, you find out that he loves his son very much, so you go and make the same request in the name of his son. Then, as a result, the rich man gives you what you have requested because he loves his son. Similarly, when we, the sinners, come before God to ask for something, He will not give it to us. But when we ask in the name of His Son, God will give it to us because He loves His Son. If this is how you understand and explain it, you are simply superstitious. Actually, if God refuses you when you ask on your own, He will also refuse you when you ask in the name of His Son.

Acts 19 gives us an account of some who superstitiously tried to imitate Paul in casting out demons in the name of the Lord Jesus. Eventually the demon said, "Jesus I know, and Paul I know; but who are ye?" and he leaped upon them and wounded them (Acts 19:15). To cast out demons in this way is simply being superstitious. When Paul cast out demons in the name of the Lord Jesus, he could say, "I am one with the Lord Jesus, and for me to live is Christ." This is the meaning and the spiritual reality of "in the name of the Lord."

II. PRAYING IN THE NAME OF THE LORD

Having understood the meaning of *being* in the name of the Lord, it becomes clear that to pray in the name of the Lord means that you, the praying one, are in union with the Lord. When you pray in the name of the Lord, the Lord prays together with you.

Brothers and sisters, when we have prayed, many times we were unable to say that we prayed in the name of the Lord, for we know that it was just our prayer; the Lord would not have prayed that way. So, at the end we should have said, "O God, we are praying in our own name," for, in practice, it is we ourselves, not the Lord praying in us. In order to be in the reality of praying in the Lord's name we need to be praying in the Lord. And when we pray thus, the Lord also prays in us.

Here we can see that the prayers in the name of the Lord in John chapters fourteen and sixteen are tremendous prayers. The Lord even says that the works which He does we will do also, and that we will do greater works than these. He also says that He will do whatever we ask in His name. This is a great matter. If you read those words in their context, you can see that the Lord Who lived on this earth has now become the Spirit living in you, and He is living Himself out from you. In the course of this living, there are many things about which you need to pray. So, while you pray, He prays in you and you in Him. When you pray in such a union with Him and He with you, you are praying in His name.

I believe, brothers and sisters, you have all had the following experience. In your early experience of praying you were able to pray for many things. But when you began to pray in the name of the Lord, immediately your prayers were reduced. When you really learn to allow the Lord to be in union with you and pray together with you, out of ten items, you may be able to pray for only three of them. You know that if you pray for the other seven things, the Lord is not praying. You are asking, but the Lord is not asking.

I have often heard children pray. At the end of their prayers they also said, "in the name of the Lord." But later on, when they really know what it means to pray in the name of the Lord, they will not be able to pray as freely as before. Neither will they be able to say "in the name of the Lord" with such ease. So, brothers, you need to be clear that to pray in the name of the Lord is not a mere formality or an empty phrase. Rather, it is that when a person lives in the Lord and is practically united with the Lord, his prayer is the Lord praying in him. In such a union many prayers become purified.

III. A LIVING OF PRAYER IN THE LORD'S NAME

Actually, John chapters fourteen through sixteen are not mainly concerned either with prayer or with life, but with a kind of united living. Here is a group of people that are chosen by God. God has separated them in order that they might be a testimony on earth, testifying that they and the Triune God have such a perfect union. This is their living. What the Lord Jesus repeatedly speaks of in those three chapters of the Bible is such a united living. A part of this living is prayer. Prayer in the name of the Lord not only needs such a living as its support and backing, but actually constitutes part of such a living. Therefore, we must know that praying in the Lord's name is not merely a matter of prayer, but even more, a matter of living. When a person lives in the Lord, by the Lord, in union with the Lord, and is mingled with the Lord, spontaneously a part of his living is prayer.

Conversely, it is not possible to pray in the name of the Lord if you do not live by the Lord or in the Lord. It is an

erroneous concept to believe that you can live apart from the
Lord and make use of His name when you have something to
ask of Him, simply because you know that your name is of no
value before Him. This is just superstitious thinking. Prayer
in the Lord's name requires a living in union with the Lord to
back it up. Prayer in the Lord's name must be a part of a
living in union with the Lord. Hence, the requirement for
such prayer is very high. It is the same as putting a name at
the end of an article to show that it is finished. What it
means is that all your daily practical living is in union with
the Lord. You learn to live before God by the risen Lord. You
walk according to His Spirit and allow His Spirit to live in
you. Such a living is the basis and support of your praying in
the Lord's name. Furthermore, such prayer actually constitutes a part of such a living.

IV. THE RELATIONSHIP BETWEEN PRAYING IN THE LORD'S NAME AND DOING GOD'S WILL

In John chapters fourteen through sixteen the Lord Jesus
clearly points out that prayers in the name of the Lord by
those who live in the Lord are prayers that accomplish God's
will. When we first heard that we needed to pray in the name
of the Lord, we thought we could pray for anything in the
Lord's name. But as we learn the lesson, we discover that out
of ten matters we want to pray for, we are able to pray for only
two. We realize that the other eight are not the Lord's will
and, therefore, the Lord cannot pray together with us. All real
prayers in the name of the Lord are surely in accordance with
God's will.

From John chapters fourteen through sixteen we can see
that doing God's will and praying in the Lord's name are
almost the same thing. When you are praying in the Lord's
name, it is equal to doing God's will. Because you are one who
lives in the Lord and by the Lord, your living is the Lord's
living. Please consider, can such a person still have goals or
inclinations outside the Lord? Of course he cannot! Therefore,
we would like to mention once again that of all the places in
the Bible that are concerned with God's promise in relation to
prayer, none seems as broad as the one here in the Gospel of

John. Here the Lord Jesus says, "Ask whatever you will, and it shall come to pass to you" (John 15:7). In one sense this promise is really broad. But actually speaking, this prayer is also very narrow, because the kind of prayer referred to in John chapters fourteen through sixteen is a prayer in the Lord. On the one hand, it says that whatever you want will be given to you, but, on the other hand, it says that such prayer needs to be in the Lord's name. Although you may have many desires when you are in yourself, once you turn and get into the Lord's name, you will see that your desires become restricted and that there are many things for which you simply cannot ask.

I remember, years ago, when I first went to Nanking, a brother invited me to a meal. He was very happy, and during the whole mealtime he was the only one talking. He kept saying, "Brother Lee, now that we have won the war, I have a feeling about this and I have a feeling about that; I would like to do this, and I would like to do that." He spoke of his many, many likes, and they were all for God. While I was listening to him, I had a very deep sensation that this brother did not know what he was saying. What he wanted, the Lord did not want. Those were *his* wants apart from the Lord. If one day he would go into the Lord, he would soon realize that he must leave all his desires outside the Lord. He himself may come into the Lord, but not his desires.

You all know what I mean. When you are living outside the Lord, you may have many desires. You may say, "I want God to do this for me and, by His power, I also want to do that for Him." But gradually, as you learn to live in the Lord, you will see that all those desires are outside the Lord and not in accordance with the will of God. Hence, God has no way to fulfill those desires. Then, and only then, can you say that your desire is God's desire. Hence, your prayer will accomplish God's will; it is doing God's will.

In summary, to pray in the name of the Lord is not just a statement or a form; rather, it is a spiritual reality and a life in union with the Lord. When we actually live in the Lord and have such a life in union with Him, we will pray spontaneously, and our prayers will surely be in accordance with the

Lord's will. When we live in Him and allow Him to live in us, He will be expressed through us. Then the prayers that come forth from us will be restricted to the expression of God's desires. Once we have this kind of prayer, God's will will definitely be accomplished because the purified desire within us issues from the mingling—the Lord with us and we with Him. The prayers of such a one are prayers in the name of the Lord.

About the Author

Witness Lee was born in 1905 in northern China and raised in a Christian family. At age 19 he was fully captured for Christ and immediately consecrated himself to preach the gospel for the rest of his life. Early in his service, he met Watchman Nee, a renowned preacher, teacher, and writer. Witness Lee labored together with Watchman Nee under his direction. In 1934 Watchman Nee entrusted Witness Lee with the responsibility for his publication operation, called the Shanghai Gospel Bookroom.

Prior to the Communist takeover in 1949, Witness Lee was sent by Watchman Nee and his other co-workers to Taiwan to ensure that the things delivered to them by the Lord would not be lost. Watchman Nee instructed Witness Lee to continue the former's publishing operation abroad as the Taiwan Gospel Bookroom, which has been publicly recognized as the publisher of Watchman Nee's works outside China. Witness Lee's work in Taiwan manifested the Lord's abundant blessing. From a mere 350 believers, newly fled from the mainland, the churches in Taiwan grew to 20,000 in five years.

In 1962 Witness Lee felt led of the Lord to come to the United States, and he began to minister in Los Angeles. During his 35 years of service in the U.S., he ministered in weekly meetings and weekend conferences, delivering several thousand spoken messages. Much of his speaking has since been published as over 400 titles. Many of these have been translated into over fourteen languages. He gave his last public conference in February 1997 at the age of 91.

He leaves behind a prolific presentation of the truth in the Bible. His major work, *Life-study of the Bible,* comprises over 25,000 pages of commentary on every book of the Bible from the perspective of the believers' enjoyment and experience of God's divine life in Christ through the Holy Spirit. Witness Lee was the chief editor of a new translation of the New Testament into Chinese called the Recovery Version and directed the translation of the same into English. The Recovery Version also appears in a number of other languages. He provided an extensive body of footnotes, outlines, and spiritual cross references. A radio broadcast of his messages can be heard on Christian radio stations in the United States. In 1965 Witness Lee founded Living Stream Ministry, a non-profit corporation, located in Anaheim, California, which officially presents his and Watchman Nee's ministry.

Witness Lee's ministry emphasizes the experience of Christ as life and the practical oneness of the believers as the Body of Christ. Stressing the importance of attending to both these matters, he led the churches under his care to grow in Christian life and function. He was unbending in his conviction that God's goal is not narrow sectarianism but the Body of Christ. In time, believers began to meet simply as the church in their localities in response to this conviction. In recent years a number of new churches have been raised up in Russia and in many European countries.

OTHER BOOKS PUBLISHED BY
Living Stream Ministry

Titles by Witness Lee:

Abraham—Called by God	978-0-7363-0359-0
The Experience of Life	978-0-87083-417-2
The Knowledge of Life	978-0-87083-419-6
The Tree of Life	978-0-87083-300-7
The Economy of God	978-0-87083-415-8
The Divine Economy	978-0-87083-268-0
God's New Testament Economy	978-0-87083-199-7
The World Situation and God's Move	978-0-87083-092-1
Christ vs. Religion	978-0-87083-010-5
The All-inclusive Christ	978-0-87083-020-4
Gospel Outlines	978-0-87083-039-6
Character	978-0-87083-322-9
The Secret of Experiencing Christ	978-0-87083-227-7
The Life and Way for the Practice of the Church Life	978-0-87083-785-2
The Basic Revelation in the Holy Scriptures	978-0-87083-105-8
The Crucial Revelation of Life in the Scriptures	978-0-87083-372-4
The Spirit with Our Spirit	978-0-87083-798-2
Christ as the Reality	978-0-87083-047-1
The Central Line of the Divine Revelation	978-0-87083-960-3
The Full Knowledge of the Word of God	978-0-87083-289-5
Watchman Nee—A Seer of the Divine Revelation ...	978-0-87083-625-1

Titles by Watchman Nee:

How to Study the Bible	978-0-7363-0407-8
God's Overcomers	978-0-7363-0433-7
The New Covenant	978-0-7363-0088-9
The Spiritual Man • 3 volumes	978-0-7363-0269-2
Authority and Submission	978-0-7363-0185-5
The Overcoming Life	978-1-57593-817-2
The Glorious Church	978-0-87083-745-6
The Prayer Ministry of the Church	978-0-87083-860-6
The Breaking of the Outer Man and the Release ...	978-1-57593-955-1
The Mystery of Christ	978-1-57593-954-4
The God of Abraham, Isaac, and Jacob	978-0-87083-932-0
The Song of Songs	978-0-87083-872-9
The Gospel of God • 2 volumes	978-1-57593-953-7
The Normal Christian Church Life	978-0-87083-027-3
The Character of the Lord's Worker	978-1-57593-322-1
The Normal Christian Faith	978-0-87083-748-7
Watchman Nee's Testimony	978-0-87083-051-8

Available at
Christian bookstores, or contact Living Stream Ministry
2431 W. La Palma Ave. • Anaheim, CA 92801
1-800-549-5164 • www.livingstream.com